SAFE CONVERSATIONS FOR WORK AND LIFE™

How to have **MENTAL HEALTH**
and **WELLBEING CONVERSATIONS**
that make a difference in someone's life

Bill Carson BSc DipMgt

First published in 2023

By Ingram Spark

© Inspire Learning Australia Pty Ltd

www.inspirelearning.au

The moral rights of the author have been asserted.

Copyright © Bill Carson 2023

Cover design and Internal design by **Fiaz Ahmed (Dezinir.99)**
Editing by **Aly Owen**

Subjects

- Leadership – mentoring and coaching
- Mental health
- Anxiety and depression signs and symptoms
- Business and personal performance

ISBN - Paperback :   978-0-6457291-0-8
ISBN - Ebook: 978-0-6457291-1-5

PRAISE FOR SAFE CONVERSATIONS FOR WORK AND LIFE™

Jurie Rossouw, author of *Executive Resilience*

"At a time when psychosocial safety and engagement are becoming increasingly crucial for organisational success, SAFE Conversations stands out as a game-changing resource. Bill's practical SAFE Conversations Framework is backed by deep dives into various mental and physical aspects, providing a highly actionable approach to cultivating a culture of psychological safety. His personal anecdotes and experiences further reinforce the book's person-centric approach, emphasising the importance of taking personal histories into account to build deep connectedness in the workplace. In short, SAFE Conversations offers an invaluable guide for anyone looking to master the art of effective communication, especially when it comes to having difficult conversations. It's a must-read for anyone seeking to develop organisations where individuals feel safe, seen, and heard at all levels."

Darren Muir, Executive General Manager, BRADKEN®

"Bradken has partnered with Bill Carson over several years, engaging him for sales training, coaching and mental health awareness programs. The SAFE Conversations book written by Bill provides the essential tools and skills for people leaders, enabling them to confidently have mental health conversations with their teams and colleagues. The book contains insights into mental health and well-being and provides the guidelines necessary to navigate safe conversations. The SAFE conversation framework is something I've personally been able to employ in the workplace."

Simone Allan, Founder, Women's Resilience Centre

"As Founder of Mondo Search, an Executive Search Firm, placing over 2800 leaders in business and now founding The Women's Resilience Centre, I care about the provision of practical hands-on programs of well-being and support for people in the workplace and at home.

Bill Carson has both lived experience, commercial experience and extensive mental health qualifications to provide practical deep insights in how to practically support people through mental health difficulties, both in the workplace and in everyday life. Bill is a servant leader who has given over 650 hours of his time to volunteer Lifeline crisis support as well. He has actively supported The Women's Resilience Centre to assist us to reset lives and positively impact generations ahead.

In SAFE Conversations for Work and Life, Bill provides a practical approach to help people be equipped in and outside the workplace and to handle managing safe and supportive conversations, supporting people to step positively forward, who are suffering mental health challenges and need solid support."

John Smibert, co-author of *The Wentworth Prospect*

"I wish this book was available when I was a manager. It's workplace mental health advice delivered in a very constructive, engaging, and relatable way.

SAFE Conversations is a wonderful workbook for Managers. It applies simple, everyday language to help managers and peers to identify mental health issues in those around them. And then provides great advice on how to provide appropriate support."

Alex Girard, National Sales Manager – ASPEN Prescription Business

"In his book, Bill provides tools and techniques that are pragmatic and simple to understand, on how to have successful SAFE conversations. These are based on research and have been tested on hundreds if not thousands of people over the years. The book is like a toolkit that all managers should always carry with them."

Dan Churches, Regional Vice President ANZ

"This book is for leaders and managers who have an awareness of mental health challenges in the workforce but don't feel they have the right skills to play their part comfortably and confidently. It has solutions, frameworks and methodologies that you can begin to learn and apply. This is a monumental effort and a commendable piece of work. Your heart and compassion and genuine intention to share your understanding, experience and insights comes through."

Mark Curry, Senior Executive, Victorian Government

"A key theme of interest to me that you address is why it is so difficult for people to open up about these sorts of problems and to seek help - and why the obverse is also true, that it's often hard for people to offer help. What your book is trying to do is to recast these existing social value judgements to facilitate rather than hinder the addressing of these issues that cause so much suffering - but it is a tough thing to do to recalibrate these norms.

I would add from my own experience that the act of sharing these feelings/ experiences with another human being who is prepared to listen to them in good faith, almost always results in an immediate sense of some relief, some reduction of the burden you've being trying to carry around on your own, and SAFE Conversations can really help with this."

Trevor McIntyre, Regional Sales Manager, BRADKEN

"Bill's key ideas in this book to change the way we think about mental health as having a positive meaning really resonates with me. As a Martial Arts instructor of over 30 years and Business Sales Manager this has changed my thinking about handling the way I deal with mental health both personally & professionally."

To Lee-Anne and
Richard
– my appreciation
and my inspiration

CONTENTS

DISCLAIMER

The information provided in this book is for educational purposes only and is not intended as a substitute for professional clinical diagnosis or treatment. This material is not intended to be used for self-diagnosis or to replace the advice of a qualified healthcare professional. If you are experiencing mental health concerns, please seek the guidance of a licensed mental health provider.

The author and publisher are not responsible for any actions or inaction, or for any loss, damage or injury, directly or indirectly, resulting from the information contained in this book.

PREFACE: MY STORY

Dr Brene Brown begins her book *The Gifts of Imperfection* with the sentiment that 'owning our story and loving ourselves through that process is the bravest thing that we will ever do'.

Can you imagine what it is like to have experienced anxiety and depression for over 30 years – and then be free?!!!

Let me briefly share with you my journey...

I have written this book because – even though as Brene shares, owning our story is hard – none of us is perfect. We are all imperfect, and we do our best to travel through this 'jungle' called life. I am not the only guide – there are hundreds – but I am playing my small part.

Ever since I was a child, I was no stranger to grief and stress, which would later evolve into depression and anxiety as a teenager.

When I was four, I had major heart surgery, and afterwards, I was chased constantly around the ward to have 44 large penicillin injections – four per day for 11 days!!!

Then, tragically, my father died in a car accident the following year. I was hugely traumatised by his death. But what made it even worse for me was that my mother was so traumatised as well. I have no memory of my mother ever consoling me in my grief because she was so consumed in her own sadness and loss.

At the time of my father's death, I was the eldest of four. My mother remarried five years later, and she had three more children. My stepfather's coping skills were severely challenged, and he would regularly react in anger and rage. I experienced a lot of physical and emotional abuse throughout my teenage years.

In my twenties I suffered from depression and contemplated suicide on more than one occasion. The anxiety had always been there. Fluctuating mood swings were a constant struggle. I would feel up, excited and motivated, and then go into my depressive, anxious cave and procrastinate for weeks on end.

My first marriage in my early 20s was also very challenging. One year into our marriage, my wife, who was a nurse, suffered a debilitating back injury when a male patient she was supporting slipped and fell on top of her. She had numerous surgeries, and unfortunately, she also developed lupus disease, and suffered immensely. She also made two suicide attempts.

My way of coping was trying to be positive. For years I constantly devoured self-help books and religious teachings to heal, along with occasional therapy sessions.

I am a 'typical guy' in that I attached a lot of shame and weakness to these aspects of my life. So, I would keep it to myself, put on a 'smiling' face, and just keep going! Most people had no idea what was really going on beneath the surface.

I had a particularly difficult time in 2014 when some client work did not go well. I had a rough time with self-blame and guilt. I was suffering from depression, anxiety and panic attacks, with mild thoughts of suicide. At this point, my struggles were significantly impacting my work – to the extent that it cost me over $100,000 of lost revenue over a nine-month period.

The Breakthrough

In May 2015, I had some 'divine intervention' and came across Dr John Gray's book *Staying Focused in a Hyper World*. It was here I first started to learn about the impact of brain chemistry on mood. I also started to learn how to heal my feelings of self-blame, shame and guilt.

A couple of months later, my current wife, Lee-Anne, went to a workshop on neuroscience and bought a book for me by Dr Daniel Amen: *Change Your Brain, Change Your Life*. I found this book to be extremely valuable, because it explained the relationship of inflammation in various parts of the brain to symptoms such as anxiety and depression.

I then embarked on a substantial research journey and read Dr William Walsh (*Nutrient Power*) and Patrick Holford (*Optimum Nutrition for the Mind*), plus many others. What I discovered from all these specialists was that symptoms may be aggravated by 'possible' inflammation in my brain and an imbalance of my brains' chemistry – as well as external triggers and stressors that I 'allowed' to impact me, and aggravate my distress.

I went on an intense personal journey of discovery and therapy about how my brain works. This journey has been tough at times – especially when noticing how I have been self-destructive and self-sabotaging in my life. However, with persistence, with therapy, and with study and research, I learnt how I can reduce the inflammation in my brain and improve both its chemical balance and the quality of my thoughts and emotions.

Freedom

Finally (as of May 2016), I was free of the emotionally painful negativity that had plagued me my entire adult life. I achieved this through several things:

1. Stabilising my brain chemistry levels so the ANT's (automatic negative thoughts) stopped crawling through my brain!
2. Training and exercising my brain on mindset and positive psychology.
3. Working with an excellent psychologist and a nutritional specialist.
4. Developing a renewed sense of purpose with the aim of making a contribution of love to humanity every day, one person at a time.

This aligns to the classic 'bio-psycho-social-logo' model in psychology and psychiatry. This model is the fundamental idea that our physical health, our mental health, our emotional health and our social health are all inter-linked. Logotherapy was founded upon the belief that striving to find meaning in life is the primary, most powerfully motivating and driving force in human beings. It was developed by neurologist and psychiatrist Dr Viktor Frankl (a survivor of the holocaust) and introduced in his most famous book, *Man's Search for Meaning* (1946).

The net result of all this research and personal development work is that I found a way to manage depression and anxiety symptoms and also function at a much higher level of my potential. I am now able to focus on my work and become the best version of myself: happy, resilient, calm and content.

I am honoured to be able to blend my professional skills and qualifications with my personal experiences to help companies, their managers and their people stay focused in a hyper world.

Everyone's journey is unique. But my story proves it is worth persisting to find the right balance and brain-training that you need to thrive professionally – and personally.

Hence for me, life is not what happens to us. Life is all about what we *do* with what happens to us. It is very much about supporting each other, helping each other, having conversations and working through our challenges to be the best version of who we can be.

I am still a 'work-in-progress'. And I always will be.

I think it's important to emphasise from the get-go that we're all continually evolving, and there's no distinct finish line in personal development, because negative emotions and situations will still always be present. It's how we're prepared to face them and manage them that shifts.

If any of the above resonates with your own experience or someone you know – then please, feel free to reach out!

A New Experience of Life and Why I Have Written This Book

As I was feeling so much better, mentally and emotionally, I decided to pay it forward. I made a big commitment of training and time to become a Lifeline volunteer telephone crisis support worker. This type of support was something that I had been wanting to do for a long time, but previously I did not have the headspace for it.

Since becoming a Lifeline volunteer, I have now done over 650 hours of answering calls for helpseekers. I am very committed to supporting others because there are so many people who are struggling and who need the social connection of someone to talk to.

Six months into the Lifeline work, my close friend Greg Dixon asked me if I would be interested in becoming a Mental Health First Aid Instructor. I am forever indebted to Greg, because this was a big turning point in my life.

Since I started this journey, I have delivered over 250 workshops to companies and communities, both face-to-face and virtual workshops.

What I have observed is that there is such an important need for leaders and managers, and people in general, to feel psychologically safe when working with others and living with others, and to know how to look out for each other.

It is important that leaders and managers notice the signs of when someone might not be at their best. They need to be empowered to be able to have a safe and caring conversation to support the other person in accessing the resources that they might need.

No shaming, no blaming, no advice-giving or stigmatising – just connecting and demonstrating that we care.

In addition to the 'human-centred' benefit of having these conversations, the business case is strong, too. Research studies have shown that a high percentage of employees feel that their manager or their company do not care about them. Similarly, a 2021 study by Achievers, an employee engagement software company, found that one in three employees in the United States do not feel valued by their employer, while one in five employees plan to leave their job in the next year. Furthermore, a 2021 report by Gallup found that only 36% of employees in the United States feel engaged in their jobs, and 13% feel actively disengaged.

Research like this in turn suggests that employees who feel valued and supported by their employer, and particularly their manager, are more engaged, productive and loyal.

The basic human need for belonging really means something!

That is why I have written this book: to help all of us develop further our person-centred communication and support skills so we can practically and authentically demonstrate that we care!

INTRODUCTION

"Mental health is the foundation for the well-being and effective functioning of individuals, families, and communities."

— World Health Organization

"Mental health is not a destination, but a journey. It's about how you drive, not where you're going."

— Noam Shpancer

Welcome to Safe Conversations for Work and Life. This book is all about helping you to have real and safe conversations that can make a difference in someone else's life.

Most managers, colleagues and people generally want to be able to help others, but they do not often know how to help. They may be concerned about saying the wrong thing, making it worse or not being able to help. This book will help you to notice the signs that someone may be struggling; how to start a conversation; what to say; what not to say; and then what resources are available to support people in the place that they are at.

You can use these conversational skills at work with your team members, if you are a leader, manager or team leader. You can also use these skills with your work colleagues, and they can also be helpful with your partner, family and friends.

My passion in writing this book is to give as many people as possible the skills and tools to have person-centred conversations.

Why Are Mental Health Conversations Often Scary?

Firstly, let us identify the many challenges that we have around having mental health conversations. There are a range of reasons why these conversations can feel so difficult, but often the thing with which we struggle the most is being afraid of saying the wrong thing.

In one survey of 25 workplaces that I conducted, this challenge was by far the most common. However, other common ones included things like 'I am afraid of making it worse' and 'I don't want to make the other person angry (with me)'.

A much broader look at the research highlights that managers are reluctant to have mental health conversations with their team members for several reasons:

1. Lack of knowledge and training
2. Fear of discrimination or bias
3. Stigma and culture of silence
4. Time and workload pressures

Why is this a Real Challenge?

The real reason talking about mental health feels so scary – whatever side of the table you're sitting on – is because of all the negativity society associates with mental health and mental illness. Despite living in a time when we're encouraged more than ever to talk about our feelings, there's still a massive amount of shame, confusion and stigma associated with these topics.

Many people avoid disclosing/discussing their mental health due to:

Stigma	What will people think of me?
Shame	What is wrong with me?
Confusion	What is happening to me? Why am I feeling this way?
Reputation	If I can't handle the pressure, then I can't do the job.
Status	What will people think of me if they find out that I have mental health issues and 'can't cope'?
Rejection	If I am struggling with my mental health, then I am weak, and I can't talk about it, for fear of being rejected.

TALKING ABOUT MENTAL HEALTH

Many people avoid disclosing/discussing their mental health due to:

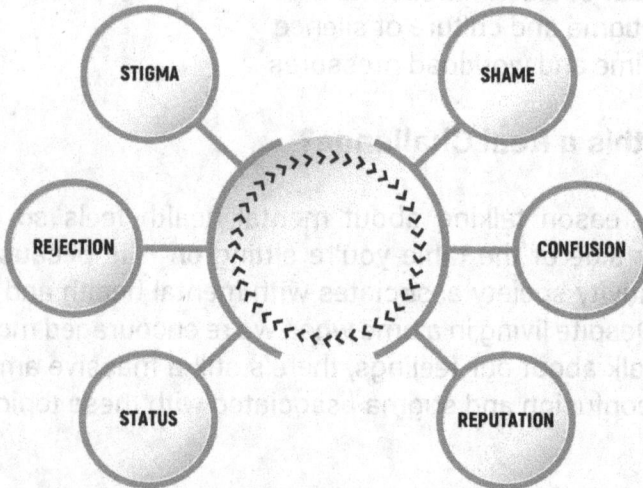

There is a key to getting past these feelings, though. And it lies with understanding that the brain is just another part of your body.

The Brain is Just Another Body Part

I often ask this question in the workshops that I run: 'Who has played competitive sport and busted a body part?'

Many people put up their hands. For example, someone might respond: 'I was 16 playing football or netball and I damaged my knee'.

Then I say to them: Imagine this. You have experienced this injury, so do you respond with 'Oh, this is so terrible; I feel so ashamed! What will people think of me? I have busted my knee, and I am in pain – I can't talk about it with others because they will think that I am weak'.

No, you do not say that. It is not the normal response!

Instead, you go to the doctor, get the injury scanned, and if required, have surgery. Then what follows is undergoing healing rehabilitation with the physiotherapist.

So, why is a mental and emotional injury any different?

Consider this list of mental and emotional injuries:

1. Divorce or relationship breakup
2. The death of someone very close to us, such as a parent, sibling, grandparent or close friend
3. Job termination (through firing or redundancy)
4. Someone else gets a promotion, pay raise or privileges that we are not given
5. We lose a lot of money, maybe from gambling or bankruptcy
6. We live in a household environment that is emotionally, physically or sexually abusive
7. Living with a disability
8. We experience significant racism, discrimination, harassment or bullying

These mental and emotional injuries are incredibly painful, but our culture does not often acknowledge the significant pain and injury complexity caused by these and other related or similar experiences.

Our culture is also very immature in talking about our emotions, which links back to all that shame, guilt etc. we carry when it comes to acknowledging and talking about our feelings and the feelings of others.

WHY IT HURTS SO MUCH

Why Does Emotional Pain Feel Like Physical Pain?

Research suggests that emotional pain, such as the pain of social rejection or loss, can activate similar areas of the brain as physical pain. Studies using brain imaging techniques such as functional magnetic resonance imaging (fMRI) have shown that areas of the brain involved in processing physical pain, such as the anterior cingulate cortex (ACC) and the insula, are also activated when people experience social rejection or exclusion.

For example, in a study published in the journal Science in 2003, researchers found that participants who had just experienced social rejection showed increased activity in the dorsal ACC, a brain region associated with the processing of physical pain. Similarly, a study published in the Proceedings of the National Academy of Sciences in 2011 found that participants who took part in a game where they were excluded by other players showed increased activity in the dorsal ACC and insula.

These findings suggest that emotional pain can be experienced in a similar way to physical pain, and that the brain processes both types of pain in overlapping neural circuits. This may help to explain why social rejection or loss can be so distressing and difficult to cope with, and why interventions that target the brain's pain processing systems, such as cognitive behavioural therapy or mindfulness meditation, can be effective in treating emotional pain

To illustrate my point, here's an example from my Lifeline [telephone crisis support] work:

A caller had been in a very painful and grieving period for five weeks following the death of her grandmother, to whom she had been very close. Her family also said they did not want anything more to do with her after the grandmother's death (for a complex range of reasons).

You can imagine the deep pain of sadness, grief and rejection she was going through. She had been drinking heavily to cope.

When I shared with her the idea of the 'brain is just another body part' and she developed the idea that this was like she had fractured her ankle – she was in pain, she was hurting – it gave her a sense of capacity for recovery. 'I can get through this', she said. 'I can go back to my psychologist, do the rehabilitation and get better over time. It is not easy, but I can do it, and I have hope. It is not me; I am not a loser. I have (the equivalent of) a fractured ankle, and I can get myself back to being in a good headspace.'

Seeing the brain as equivalent to just another body part was very transforming and helpful for her.

Comparison of the physical and the mental/emotional

If you look at the table below, you can see the relationship of physical illness (body-based illness) to physical health challenges, physical fitness and physical performance. It shows the many physical situations we can find ourselves in.

Ideally, we want to have more of 3C and 4D but physical illnesses, injuries and health challenges will happen in our lives.

COMPARISON OF THE PHYSICAL &
THE MENTAL-EMOTIONAL

1A. Physical Illness [Body-based illness]	Asthma, Bronchitis, Colitis, Cancer, Heart disease, Diabetes	*Treatment by Medical Specialist –Respiratory, Gastrointestinal, Oncologist*
2B. Physical Health Challenges, Problems & Injuries	Cold, Flu, Hayfever, Ulcer, Back pain, Injury such as broken ankle	*Treatment by Doctor, Physiotherapist Physical First Aid*
3C. Physical Health & Fitness	Gym, Exercise, Nutrition, Wellbeing, Pilates, Yoga & Work Skills	*Personal Trainer, Nutritionist, Naturopath Work Skills Training*
4D. Physical Performance & Potential	Swimming, Cycling, Running, Football, Surfing, Business Performance	*Sports Trainers and Coaches*
1A. Mental Illness [Brain-based illness]	Post Traumatic Stress Disorder, Major Depressive Disorder, Major Anxiety Disorder, Schizophrenia, Suicidal thoughts, Drug-induced Psychosis	*Treatment by Psychiatrist, Clinical Psychologist*
2B. Mental Health Challenges, Problems & Injuries	Stress, Anxiety, Depression, Negative Thinking, Death of Loved one, Domestic Violence, Addictions – food, alcohol, drugs, gambling, porn	*Treatment by Doctor, Clinical Psychologist, Counsellor Mental Health First Aid*
3C. Mental Health & Fitness	Mental Fitness and Resilience Skills, Wellbeing strategies, Happiness strategies	*Mental Fitness & Resilience Skills Training & Coaching*
4D. Mental Performance & Potential	Business and sport performance	*High Performance Trainers, Coaches & Psychologists*

You can see similar comparisons for mental illness (brain-based illness) to mental health challenges, mental fitness and mental performance.

In a similar way, our preference would be more of 3C and 4D to enjoy life by being mentally and emotionally healthy and well.

But we ALL experience many challenges throughout our lives that can create significant mental and emotional difficulties for us.

As smart, intelligent human beings, it is important that we be kind and compassionate to ourselves and each other and recognise that we all have difficulties at various times in our lives. It would be very helpful if we all stopped the stigma and ignorance associated with all things to do with the 'mental' and the 'emotional'!!!

Who Has This Book Been Written For?

a. Corporate Focus

This book has been written for people leaders, human resource managers, safety managers, line managers and team leaders – anyone who is responsible for managing people and looking to promote a more proactive, safe working culture when it comes to employee well-being.

The COVID-19 pandemic has had a significant impact on people's mental health and well-being, and this impact has been reflected in the number of stress-related insurance claims that have been made.

According to data from the Australian Prudential Regulation Authority (APRA), there was a 12% increase in total claims paid out for mental health-related conditions between March and September 2020 compared to the same period in 2019. This includes claims related to stress, anxiety and depression. In addition, a survey conducted by the Australian Bureau of Statistics (ABS) in May 2020 found that four in ten Australians reported feeling more stressed than usual as a result of the pandemic. This stress was particularly true for those who had experienced job loss or financial hardship.

Human resource managers are experiencing the full brunt of the pressure to reduce the number of claims being lodged and assist their teams. People and culture leaders are likewise looking for expanded ways to leverage people skills and capabilities for both managers and team leaders, as well as team members, across the organisation.

Companies increasingly operate in complex work environments that involve on-site or hybrid ways of working. The mental and emotional health of all team members are constantly being impacted by the turbulent demands, changes and challenges that we all experience in business today.

Hence, there is an increasing demand for managers to build their own skills to have mental health and well-being conversations with their team members. Much of the existing training in this area is basic mental health awareness, which does very little to upskill the manager/team leader in the advanced communication skills that are needed to engage safely in these conversations. Some managers in the past have questioned whether it is even within their remit to have these conversations.

However, the new Code of Practice for Managing Psychosocial Hazards is now making it a WHS (Work, Health and Safety) requirement for all managers, in all workplaces, in all states of Australia. Internationally this practice aligns with the new safety standard of ISO 45003 Guidelines for Managing Psychosocial Risks.

ISO 45003:2021 - GUIDELINES FOR MANAGING PSYCHOSOCIAL RISKS

- ISO 45003 is a new international standard on occupational health and safety (OH&S) published by the International Organization for Standardization (ISO) in 2021. The standard provides guidance for organizations on how to manage psychosocial risks and promote mental well-being in the workplace.

- It is intended to complement existing OH&S management standards, such as ISO 45001, which focuses on the management of physical risks in the workplace. The new standard recognizes that work-related psychosocial hazards, such as work-related stress, harassment, and bullying, can have significant impacts on employee mental health, job satisfaction, and productivity.

- This standard provides a framework for identifying and assessing psychosocial risks in the workplace, and for developing strategies to manage and mitigate those risks. It also emphasizes the importance of involving workers and their representatives in the process of managing psychosocial risks, and of promoting a culture of openness and support for mental well-being in the workplace.

- Overall, ISO 45003 is designed to help organizations take a proactive and preventative approach to managing psychosocial risks and promoting mental well-being in the workplace, with the goal of creating healthier and more productive working environments.

b. Personal Focus

This book is also for everyone at a personal level if you want to help someone because:

- you have seen significant changes in their mental and/or emotional states.
- they have become more worried about things than they normally would be.
- they are more stressed, snappy, angry or constantly finding fault with others.
- they are more fearful and putting themselves down more often.

- you are noticing that someone is using substances and behaviours more frequently to cope – such as with increases in eating, drinking, drugs, shopping, porn, gaming and gambling.

All these areas are indicators that someone may be experiencing mental health challenges.

c. You are Not Being Taught to be a Therapist or Advice-giver

The important thing here is that we are NOT teaching you how to become a therapist, a problem solver, or an advice-giver. There are two main reasons for that:

1. This is not your area of expertise.
2. No-one likes being told what to do in personal matters.

This book is all about how we guide and support somebody to become self-aware of what would be most useful and helpful for them, and to help them through what it is that they are going through.

It is about helping you be brave enough to start conversations that matter and make a difference in someone's life. Not try to 'fix' it as you see fit.

When we help others, it is a gift that we give to another human to connect with them. When we are supportive, we are validating what they are going through, and then we help them to identify resources and support that can help and empower them.

What This Book Will Cover

This book will give you the confidence and the competence to have a safe conversation with someone that you care about, or whose performance/behaviour is impacting you.

These conversations need to be safe for you and the other person. In most workplaces, families and cultures, it is not safe to talk about how we feel, because the risk is we will be shamed and blamed. As we mentioned before, the reason why this happens is that most people do not know how to respond to another person's difficult feelings, and they therefore respond in hurtful and dysfunctional ways. This happens because they have never been taught how to respond appropriately.

So, first, in Chapter 1, we will dive into identifying what the signs and symptoms would be if someone is struggling with mental and emotional health difficulties. To go back to our physical health analogy, it might be very easy to see someone is in a moon boot for a fractured ankle, but there are plenty of physical illnesses that aren't easily visible. If someone has an internal illness, such as an ulcerated colon, and they are experiencing abdominal pain, you can't see it! Similarly, when people are experiencing mental and emotional injuries, they feel mental and emotional pain, and it shows up in specific ways – which we need to recognise and understand, and then stop being cynical and judgmental.

How do you tell the difference between personal issues and performance issues? Many managers and companies get this wrong, and it has damaging consequences – to people, productivity and profits.

If you are an action learner and you want to get straight into the 'how-to', then I suggest you read Chapter 1 and then read Chapter 4. But, just be aware that if your mental health awareness is low, you need Chapters 2 and 3.

If you are a context reader, you might prefer to read the chapters sequentially.

In Chapter 2 we look at why mental and emotional difficulties happen to some people and less to others. We also look at the definitions of mental health and what is mental illness before exploring the big stressors at work and in life and the impact that these can have.

This is a very important chapter if you do not know much about mental health and mental illness. For example, some people say the youth of today are not as 'tough' as they used to be, and we look at the fallacy of this perspective.

In Chapter 3 we explore why it can be difficult to connect and have these conversations. Managers exist to solve problems in companies and tell people what to do, and many managers want to be helpful and give advice.

But this advice is counterintuitive – and a massive brain-fry for most managers, who think they must 'solve' the 'problems', particularly if someone's personal issues are impacting their own and/or the team's performance.

However, what we must learn is that it's best practice to empower people struggling with personal challenges to access their own resources, or professional resources – not try to be the problem-solver or the advice-giver.

In Chapter 4 we dive into the actual SAFE Conversation Skills Framework and teach you how to have person-centred conversations, which are different from task-focused and performance conversations. These new skills will enhance and expand your leadership and management communication skills. Here you will also learn how to assist (appropriately) team members, colleagues and friends who might be struggling with mental and emotional difficulties or unwellness.

You will learn a best practice and evidenced-based method to engage in a compassionate, person-centred conversation to empower the person to develop self-awareness of their own situation and help them identify the resources that will be most helpful for them.

Remember, unless you are a trained and qualified therapist or doctor, you should not be thinking that you need to problem-solve or give advice – even with the best of intentions.

S.A.F.E CONVERSATIONS FOR WORK AND LIFE™

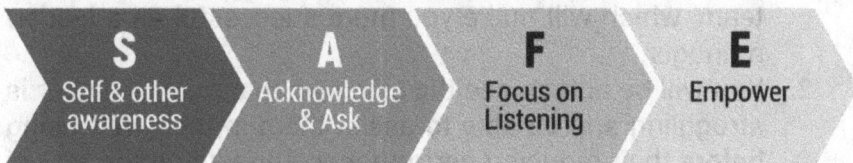

S	A	F	E
Self & other awareness	Acknowledge & Ask	Focus on Listening	Empower

TASK-FOCUSED CONVERSATIONS

PERSON-CENTRED CONVERSATIONS

In Chapter 5 we cover how you can assist someone you care about – including yourself. Here we identify a broad range of self-care and professional-care approaches and strategies. This chapter will be valuable in teaching you how to live a happier life, and how you can support others in doing the same.

In Chapter 6 we give you guidance if you are concerned about someone who is deeply struggling with their difficult thoughts – such as thoughts of suicide.

What's In It For You?

So, what are the benefits of these conversations? What is the value to you in and beyond the workplace?

1. You will contribute to creating a happier and more engaged team, which will make you more successful as a leader/manager.
2. You will be able to see the signs when a team member is struggling and be able to assist them in their well-being before their reducing performance impacts on the rest of the team.
3. You will increase your professional skill set in having difficult conversations that empower your team members rather than disempower them.
4. You will be seen as a leader/manager who authentically cares about your people and their well-being, not just someone who is self-focused on your own results and KPIs.
5. You will be a partner, friend and family member who will learn to be more supportive and less judgmental or fearful in having a caring conversation, and you will minimise feeling like you have to provide answers or give advice.

CHAPTER 1

THE SIGNS – THAT SOMEONE IS STRUGGLING

"You don't have to be positive all the time. It's perfectly okay to feel sad, angry, annoyed, frustrated, scared, or anxious. Having feelings doesn't make you a negative person. It makes you human."

– Lori Deschene

Most leaders, managers, and people in general do not know how to handle mental and emotional unwellness in others, nor in themselves.

There is an enormous amount of stigma, lack of understanding and lack of empathy/willingness to learn. One of the things that I am hugely passionate about is for us as humans to become so much more informed and educated about our brains and bodies – about how we think and how we feel – and then be able to deal with the increasing complexity that life on planet Earth is delivering up for us these days.

What are the Signs and Symptoms that Someone Might be Struggling with Mental and Emotional Unwellness?

There would be a range of behavioural challenges for the person that you may observe, and **noticing the changes** is the most important thing that we can do. This is what I am going to be encouraging as we progress forward.

You might notice behavioural changes like:

- They are withdrawing from others.
- They are having more frequent bouts of being cranky, angry or frustrated, or appear to have more conflict than usual.
- Reduced participation in work activities.
- An increase in errors or accidents. This situation is particularly prevalent in manufacturing and construction type environments.
- A lack of concentration and having difficulty with their memory.
- They are behaving extra perkily or working excessively.
- Sudden mood swings.
- They appear to have lost their self-confidence.
- They are off their game in terms of their normal level and quality of work performance.
- They are procrastinating about getting work done, have uncompleted projects or are frequently running behind schedule.
- Their usual decisiveness in situations is lacking.
- They are expressing an excessive degree of fear or worry.

Physically speaking, when someone is struggling, you might notice changes like:

- Complaining frequently of feeling tired, exhausted, and run down.
- Getting sick a lot (immune systems tend to be more fragile when someone is under persistent stress).
- Having a disheveled appearance.
- Frequent headaches.
- Persistent and resistant muscle pains.
- Moving more slowly.
- Changes in sleep patterns.
- Weight loss or weight gain.
- Gastrointestinal problems.

Signs and Symptoms that Employees May Be Struggling with Work Performance

Any mental and emotional health challenges and any subsequent behavioural and physical changes may have a knock-on effect on work performance, such as the quality of their work, their ability to meet deadlines or increases in absenteeism. The following chart outlines some of the potential effects on work performance. We may also see increases in bullying, harassment, blaming others, lack of cooperation or being actively disengaged.

MENTAL HEALTH AND WORK PERFORMANCE

Signs and symptoms that employees are struggling can appear in the work context through:

INCREASED LATENESS/ ABSENCE

LOW MORALE

LACK OF COOPERATION

DECREASED PRODUCTIVITY

INCREASED ACCIDENTS/ INCIDENTS

FREQUENT FATIGUE

POOR CONCENTRATION/ MEMORY

MISSED DEADLINES

DECREASED INVOLVEMENT

Key Aspects of Mental Health Safety in the Workplace

The big problem is that most managers and team members do not know how to respond appropriately to people when they are struggling with any of these challenges. Many work environments are not mentally safe for the individual nor psychologically safe for the team members.

Mental health safety in the workplace is demonstrated by continually and consistently demonstrating conditions and practices that support employees' mental health and wellbeing. It involves creating a work environment that promotes positive mental health and provides resources and support for those who may be struggling.

KEY ASPECTS OF MENTAL HEALTH SAFETY IN THE WORKPLACE

1 **Clear policies and procedures:** Employers should have clear policies and procedures in place that promote mental health and address issues such as workplace stress, harassment, and discrimination. These policies should be communicated to all employees and regularly reviewed to ensure they are effective.

2 **Supportive leadership:** Leaders and managers should be trained to recognize the signs of mental health issues and provide appropriate support and resources to employees. They should also encourage an open and supportive culture where employees feel comfortable discussing mental health concerns.

3 **Employee resources:** Employers should provide resources and support for employees, such as an Employee Assistance Program (EAP), counselling services, and access to mental health resources and information.

4 **Work-life balance:** Employers should promote work-life balance and provide flexibility when possible to help employees manage their mental health and personal responsibilities.

5 **Training and education:** Employers should provide training and education to all employees on mental health awareness and how to support colleagues who may be struggling.

Overall, creating a workplace that prioritizes mental health safety can lead to increased employee engagement, productivity, and overall job satisfaction.

In work environments where there is no mental health safety or low team psychological safety, or where there are no mental health first aiders, there is no safety for the employees. When their personal difficulties have a negative effect on their own performance and impact on others in the team or company, they do not feel safe to discuss their issues.

Most leaders and managers do not know how to handle these situations with their team members. In many instances, they aggravate the situation, or they neglect it as they are not equipped to handle the situation. For example, if a manager/team leader has no experience with mental health themselves, they may focus on the work performance 'issue' and fail to acknowledge that mental health challenges may be the cause.

So in these environments, frequently the discussion turns into a performance management issue when it should not be.

Recently a friend of mine shared how he pushed back on both the workload he was experiencing and not getting support from other managers in the division. His senior leader's response was: 'Mark, I am not interested in your feelings; I want facts.'

This reaction is entirely inappropriate, and it is not helpful to the person who is asking for support. It also plays into the great fallacy in corporate life that sees the 'rational' mind as supreme and the 'emotional' mind is weak and unstable – what human being ever has thoughts without feelings and emotions?!

It is a far better outcome for both team performance and the business to have managers and team members appropriately trained in mental health safety, including knowing how to connect (safely and with care) with someone who is struggling and have the mental health conversations that will help the person.

Remember the important caveat here: mental health support doesn't mean becoming an advice-giver, therapist or best buddy.

Another critically important aspect of mental health safety in the workplace is that we learn to safe-guard ourselves.

You don't want to say the wrong thing or make their situation worse, but you also do not want to become the go-to person for someone else's personal challenges – it's not your job, and you are not a trained counsellor or even an 'accidental counsellor'. You will learn 'how to put on your own oxygen mask first' in Chapter 4.

Another friend of mine, Jenny, once shared: 'I often became the mental health advocate for others at work who weren't even in my immediate team (because most others were scared or unequipped to), and while I absolutely wanted to do that, at one point I was doing so much of it for so many people and taking on others' pain that it was a bit like "put the oxygen mask on yourself first" – I became emotionally exhausted and I had to look after myself so I could support both myself and others.'

CHAPTER 2

THE CAUSES – WHY CAN MENTAL HEALTH DIFFICULTIES HAPPEN?

"Mental health needs a great deal of attention. It's the final taboo and it needs to be faced and dealt with."
– Adam Ant

Author's note:

The information provided here is for educational purposes only and is not intended as a substitute for professional clinical diagnosis or treatment. This material is not intended to be used for self-diagnosis or to replace the advice of a qualified healthcare professional. If you are experiencing mental health concerns, please seek the guidance of a licensed mental health provider.

If this material triggers some uncomfortable emotions for you, then we encourage you please to seek appropriate support. This support could be with a family member, friend, colleague or a helpline such as Beyond Blue (on 1300 22 4636), Lifeline (on 13 11 14), your Employee Assistance Provider or your doctor.

Additional author's note:

Please also note that this chapter provides a broad overview of the complex potential causes of mental health difficulties with the aim of generating greater mental health awareness. Some readers might be interested in this background context. If you are not, or you're already familiar with these topics, then skip to Chapter 3 and Chapter 4. You may want to come back to this chapter later on.

Now, without further ado: what are some potential causes of mental health difficulties? Let us dive into the causes and triggers, and give ourselves a good understanding of the complications in life that can contribute to significant mental and emotional health difficulties, challenges and problems.

I have often had managers say to me: 'Why does it happen, and how do I tell the difference between someone who is "pulling the mental health card" as an excuse versus someone who has a diagnosable mental health condition that they are dealing with?'

First let's define what is 'mental health' and what is 'mental illness/injury'.

These two terms are on the same continuum, but they are different terms. Take a look at the graphic below.

THE MENTAL HEALTH AND MENTAL ILLNESS/INJURY CONTINUUM

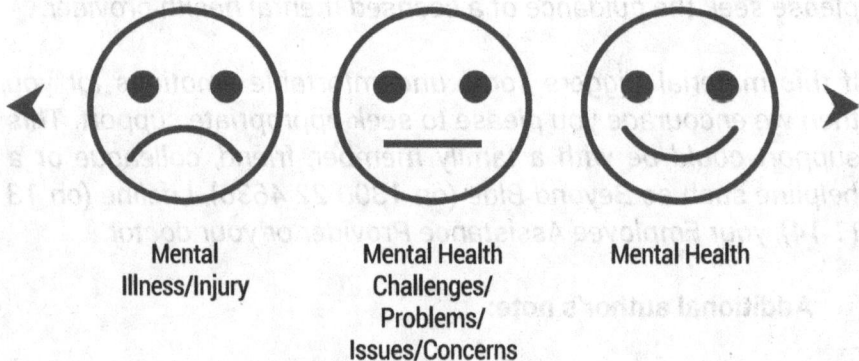

| Mental Illness/Injury | Mental Health Challenges/ Problems/ Issues/Concerns | Mental Health |

Source: 2019 Standard Mental Health First Aid Instructor Teaching Notes, p.14

On the right-hand side, we have positive mental health, and then at the left end of the continuum, we have mental illness and injuries. In the middle are the challenges, problems and difficulties to overcome. I will cover the numbers associated with these shortly.

We all sit somewhere along this continuum, and our mental and emotional health varies from day to day, week to week and over the course of our lives depending on our experiences, coping skills, biology and access to support services.

What is Mental Health?

In theory, mental health is the same as happiness and the same as well-being, and this equivalence is important for us to understand. But different people will give them different meanings.

According to the World Health Organization, mental health is defined as a state of well-being and happiness in which a person:

1. has positive relationships;
2. realises their potential;
3. copes with the normal stresses of life;
4. works productively; and
5. is able to make a contribution to their community.

[Mental Health First Aid Manual, p.4, 4th Edition, March 2022]

One thing we need to stop doing in our culture is stigmatising 'mental health'. For example, it is not uncommon that we might look at someone and say, 'They have physical health', with the implied adjective here being that they have 'good' physical health.

But what we might often hear in a different situation is, 'Oh, they've got mental health!' The implied adjective here is 'poor' mental health.

Mental health is a good thing, just like physical health is a good thing. However, as we could have physical health challenges (with our backs, stomachs or hearts), similarly we could have mental health challenges (like anxiety, anger or depression).

There are a wide range of things that we can do in our lives to help us improve our mental health/happiness/well-being.

- Creating positive relationships through demonstrating gratitude and appreciation.
- Using your full potential by doing the work that you are really meant to be doing, and living a life of purpose and meaning, whatever that means to you.
- Developing strategies to cope with the normal stresses of life.
- Building approaches and habits that ensure good nutrition, exercise and sleep.
- Being productive both in work and in your personal life.
- Making contributions to the lives of others that have a positive impact for both you and them.

These mental health boosters will vary for everyone, and sometimes our life circumstances can be very challenging, which may hinder our ability to put these into practice.

What Is Mental Illness or Mental Injury?

Again, according to the World Health Organization, mental illness is a diagnosable condition that causes major changes to thoughts, feelings and behaviour; impairs functioning; and is persistent over time (*Mental Health First Aid Manual, p.4, 4th Edition, March 2022*).

So, what separates having a bad hair day or experiencing moments of anxiety, anger or grief from a diagnosable mental health condition?

Think in terms of D.I.S: **D**uration, **I**mpact, and **S**everity.

Duration: Has the person been experiencing mental/emotional difficulties for extended periods of time (e.g. at least several weeks, if not longer)?

Impact: Is their mental health condition impacting on their life, work or relationships?

Severity: Has the person experienced any traumatic situations?

Source: 2019 Standard Mental Health First Aid Instructor Teaching Notes, p.14

Please keep in mind that these definitions are not meant to be diagnostic, but indicative. Please consult your licensed healthcare professional if you might be concerned about yourself or someone else.

Let us view these terms in the context of a physical illness.

The difference between my having a niggly lower back pain and significant pain that needs treatment would firstly involve the duration of the pain. Does it happen every so often, or is it something acute and persistent?

The impact of this pain might be that it is difficult for me to sleep, do my job or go about my daily life, and I might be grumpy and challenging to live with!

The severity might be related to the nature of the injury – is it a strained muscle, disc degeneration or acute, traumatic back injury?

If that niggly pain gets worse over time or if I strain it further and it changes to consistent, stabbing pain, then I would go to the doctor – or the chiropractor, physiotherapist, etc. – to help me deal with it.

> Mental illness/injury is a health problem that significantly impacts many people, and how we think, behave, and interact.
>
> [Mental Health First Aid Manual, p.4, 4th Edition March 2022]

The same can happen with a mental/emotional illness or injury.

Consider the example of a long-term relationship that breaks up.

In many instances, this breakup will cause considerable sadness, grief and maybe depression.

This low mood might continue for an extended period and start to impact on work, relationships and living life.

The severity might increase due to issues of child(ren) access, increasing work pressures or other significant life stressors and post-breakup adjustments.
If this happens, then we must follow the same guidelines for our mental health as we would with our physical health: if symptoms persist, please see your health care professional.

Many people stigmatise themselves with their own mental and emotional health difficulties. They may say things like:

- I don't want to talk to anyone about it. What can they do to help, anyway? (This is as silly as thinking that if you had a fractured ankle you wouldn't go to a doctor!)
- It will cost me too much. (Please consider using free helplines like Lifeline and Beyond Blue, as well as speaking to your doctor or counsellor about more affordable resources. There is always a way to get help.)

There are many different types and degrees of mental illnesses or injuries. A few examples include:

- Severe Anxiety Disorder: severe anxiety that continues for an extended period of time and has a significant impact on your life.
- Major Depressive Disorder: significant sadness and grief (often from losses or changes to life circumstances) that translate to persistent low moods over an extended period of time.

- Substance use disorders: the use of the substance impacts on relationships, the capacity for work or looking after oneself.
- Psychosis: symptoms of delusions and hallucinations that can occur with significant brain-based illness and head injuries.

Covering specific mental health illnesses and injuries in detail is beyond the scope of this book, but if you want to know more about these disorders, you can find more detail in a Mental Health First Aid Accreditation Training course – details in Chapter 7 – Summary and Options

As always, if you are concerned that you or someone you know is affected by potential mental illness or injury, please consult your licensed healthcare professional.

What Are the Statistics for Mental Illness in Australia?

According to a study completed in 2007 by the Australian Bureau of Statistics, out of the 8,841 people (aged 18–65) surveyed:

- 20% of Australians aged 18-65 experience a diagnosable mental illness in any one year. Over the course of a lifetime, on average, about half of us will experience a mental illness. I will explain that a bit more as we go, but it's worth noting that a lot of people do not access treatment, so this number is still likely quite low compared to reality. Likewise, more recently (and post-COVID-19), more people are accessing treatment, but still, any numbers captured are likely much lower than the reality.
- One in three women and one in five men experience anxiety disorders.
- One in five women and one in eight men experience depressive disorders.
- Substance use is much higher in males than in females.

THE STATISTICS

20%

Of Australians aged 18-65 experience a diagnosable mental illness in any year

45%

Of Australians will experience mental illness in their lifetime

54%

Don't access treatment

ANXIETY DISORDERS

Affects 1 in 3 women and 1 in 5 men

DEPRESSIVE DISORDERS

Affects 1 in 5 women and 1 in 8 men

SUBSTANCE USE DISORDERS

7.0% Males and 3.3% Females

7.0%   3.3%

9 AUSTRALIANS COMMIT SUICIDE EVERY DAY - 7 MEN & 2 WOMEN

Source: Australian Bureau of Statistics, National Survey of Mental Health and Wellbeing 2007

Author's note: For the purposes of this book, these numbers are intended to give an idea of the average experience of mental health illness in Australia; they are not intended to be all-inclusive and representative of the entire population and individual communities. If the reader has a more detailed interest in the experiences of specific populations (such as the LGBTIQIA+

community, Aboriginal and Torres Strait Islanders, racial or ethnic groups, etc) then please consult more inclusive and relevant research sources.

Why such a difference between men and women?

Putting aside the challenge with most existing research (in that it fails to account for non-binary and fluid gender identities), you could easily argue that societal conditioning and the complexities of gender identity contribute to this difference. As a society, we're often taught that mental illness is a 'weakness' or it's 'our fault', and men or male-presenting people are often highly discouraged from connecting with their feelings from a very young age. While this attitude is changing, men are still often told to 'suck it up' or 'get on with it' and 'be a man' because 'boys don't cry'.

Regardless of gender identity or expression, when we experience difficult childhood stresses and trauma, as well as additional stresses in adolescence and beyond, then we are generally encouraged to bottle it up and stuff those feelings and emotions into our bodies. So if, as a male, you have been subscribed to extra conditioning about avoiding emotional communication, then you may be more likely to try to cope with things like substances and behaviours to numb the emotions.

What about data by age?

More recent Australian Bureau of Statistics data (via the National Study of Mental Health and Well-Being in 2020–2021) showcases how different age groups and gender identities experienced reported mental illness during that year.

ALL 12-MONTH MENTAL HEALTH DISORDERS BY AGE & GENDER IN AUSTRALIA, 2020 - 21

Any 12-month mental disorder, by age and sex, 2020 - 21

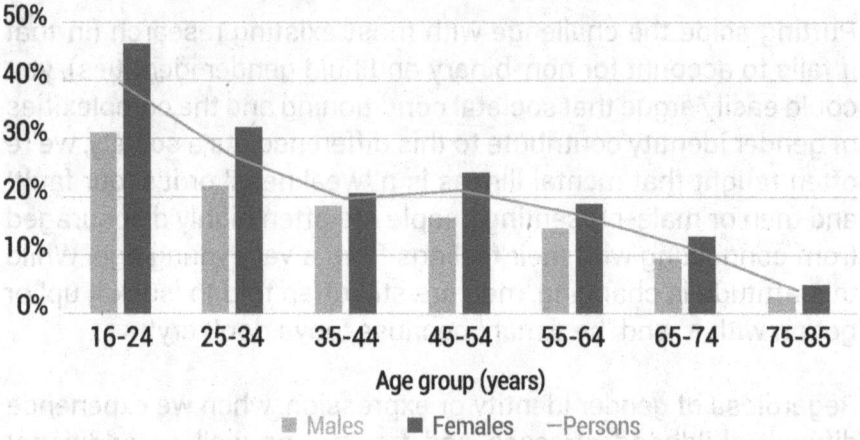

Source: Australian Bureau of Statistics, National Study of Mental Health and Wellbeing 2020-21

These results show that a lot of younger people – in particular, young women –are really struggling with mental and emotional health difficulties for a wide complex range of reasons, likely including but not limited to things like social media exposure, climate crises, negative media coverage, the cost of living crisis, infringes on civil liberties with respect to gender and sexual identity, etc. These are high numbers for young people, who are particularly vulnerable to mental and emotional health difficulties. I will explain that shortly in the section on 'The Stress Reaction'.

How Do These Figures Show Up in the Workplace?

WHERE ARE YOU AND YOUR TEAM?

The Wellbeing Continuum Impacted by the Pandemic & Change & Ongoing Challenges

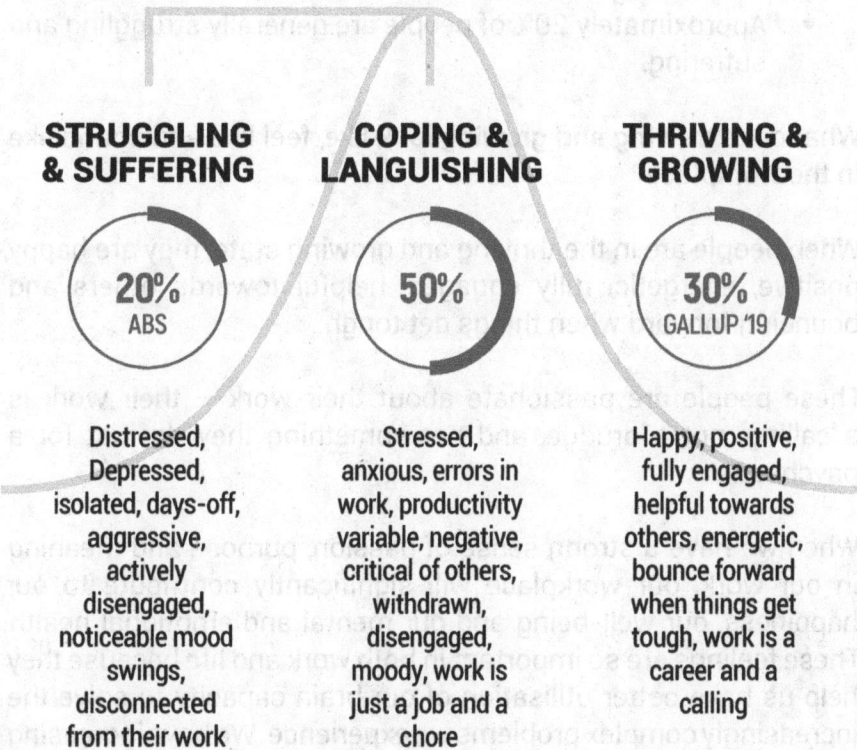

STRUGGLING & SUFFERING	COPING & LANGUISHING	THRIVING & GROWING
20% ABS	**50%**	**30%** GALLUP '19
Distressed, Depressed, isolated, days-off, aggressive, actively disengaged, noticeable mood swings, disconnected from their work	Stressed, anxious, errors in work, productivity variable, negative, critical of others, withdrawn, disengaged, moody, work is just a job and a chore	Happy, positive, fully engaged, helpful towards others, energetic, bounce forward when things get tough, work is a career and a calling

The above diagram proposes an overview of how mental health difficulties and unwellness show up in the work environment and in life.

We see three broad categories of how people are engaging in their work on this mental health and well-being continuum. According to Gallup and the Australian Bureau of Statistics, we can identify these three broad categories as:

- Approximately 30% of people are generally thriving and growing.
- Approximately 50% of people are generally coping and languishing.
- Approximately 20% of people are generally struggling and suffering.

What does **thriving and growing** look like, feel like and sound like in the workplace?

When people are in the thriving and growing state, they are happy, positive, energetic, fully engaged, helpful towards others and bouncing forward when things get tough.

These people are passionate about their work – their work is a calling, not a drudge, and not something they do just for a paycheque!

When we have a strong sense of passion, purpose and meaning in our work, our workplace will significantly contribute to our happiness, our well-being and our mental and emotional health. These feelings are so important in both work and life because they help us have better utilisation of our brain capacity to solve the increasingly complex problems we experience. We have increasing capacity to resist the negative – we have more resilience!

What does **coping, struggling or suffering** look like, sound like and feel like?

We have seen earlier what signs and symptoms might appear when someone is struggling or suffering (or starting to struggle or suffer).

POSSIBLE EARLY SIGNS

BEHAVIORAL

1. CHANGES IN BEHAVIOUR
2. CONFLICT WITH TEAM MEMBERS/MANAGER
3. WITHDRAWING FROM OTHERS
4. NOT GETTING THINGS DONE
5. INCREASED ERRORS, ACCIDENTS
6. EXCESSIVE FEAR OR WORRY
7. REDUCED PARTICIPATION IN WORK ACTIVITIES
8. LOSS OF CONFIDENCE
9. INABILITY TO CONCENTRATE
10. INDECISIVE
11. DIFFICULTY WITH MEMORY

PHYSICAL

1. CONSTANT TIREDNESS
2. FEELING SICK AND RUN DOWN
3. DISHEVELLED APPEARANCE
4. PERSISTENT/RESISTANT MUSCLE ACHES AND PAINS
5. GASTRO-INTESTINAL PROBLEMS
6. CHANGES IN SLEEP PATTERNS
7. WEIGHT LOSS OR GAIN
8. MOVING MORE SLOWLY OR APPEARING AGITATED
9. HEADACHES

The recent pandemic has had a significant impact on mental health globally. Many individuals have experienced increased stress, anxiety, and depression due to factors like social isolation, economic hardship and uncertainty about the future. According to a survey by the Center for Disease Control and Prevention (CDC) in the United States, the percentage of adults with symptoms of anxiety or depressive disorder increased from 36.4% to 41.5%

between August 2020 and February 2021, and 70% reported that they were struggling or suffering. Similar trends have been reported in other developed countries, like Canada, the United Kingdom, and Australia.

The pandemic has also highlighted existing mental health disparities and inequalities, particularly in developed countries. Some populations, including healthcare workers, individuals from lower socioeconomic backgrounds, and those with pre-existing mental health conditions have been especially affected.

Governments, mental health organisations and healthcare providers have responded to the increased demand for mental health services by offering more resources, such as teletherapy and online support groups. However, the long-term impact of the pandemic on mental health is still uncertain, and further research is needed to fully understand the implications.

There is also a rise in the workplace around psychological injury claims. SafeWork New South Wales conducted an analysis looking at these claims over two different periods (2014–2015 and 2018–2019). Comparing and averaging the two date ranges:

- There was a 53% increase in claims for psychological injury since 2015, whereas physical injury claims only increased by 3.5%.
- The average length of time off work was 175 days for psychological claims, compared to 44 days for physical injury claims.
- The cost of those claims was $585 million, with the average claim being over $85,000, compared to the average physical claims of $21,000.
- 26,600 workers needed time off, which meant an overall collective average estimate of 1.2 million days lost.

The introduction of new work health and safety legislation into workplaces in Australia in April 2023 is focused on reducing the psychosocial hazards in the workplace. The aim is to reduce and mitigate the mechanisms of injury, such as work harassment and/or workplace bullying (responsible for 35% of psychological injuries), work pressures (28% of psychological injuries), workplace or occupational violence (10% of psychological injuries), and exposure to traumatic events (8% of psychological injuries).

The Stress/Threat Reaction – at the Personal-Social Level

A stressor is any activity, event, or other stimulus that causes stress.

The first thing to understand is that we as humans have a physical stress reaction and a need to survive and thrive. In fact, every species on the planet needs to survive and thrive.

To achieve this 'survive and thrive' state, the basic stress reaction response activates the three Fs:

1. Fight
2. Flight
3. Freeze

However, humans are different, and our responses are more nuanced than these three ingrained instincts and physical responses!

As the highly advanced and social mammals that we are, we take the stress reaction of fight, flight or freeze to another level. It's not just physical for us; we apply it at a personal and social level, too.

For example, imagine that you are driving along the highway and someone cuts in front of you. In that moment, from a physical survival perspective, your whole system will react in a nanosecond – you hit the brakes and protect yourself. However, the next thing that happens is that we take it to a social level, which is often something like: 'How dare you – you f..!@#*! idiot!' In other words, we apply the stress reaction at the personal-social level.

In the workplace, these potential stressors are numerous. Here are some examples:

1. You put in a big effort to help your boss and your team to meet an important milestone, and then nothing – no thanks, no recognition, no celebration, just another 'critically important' project/client.
2. A major change is being rolled out, and there is a lot of uncertainty and confusion. You ask questions to find out why and how, and you are told that you are disruptive and uncooperative.
3. You share an idea with a boss or colleague, and they take it and share it with others as if it was their idea, without giving you the credit, and you feel betrayed.
4. People talk about you behind your back, or they scapegoat you for something going wrong in a project.
5. You find out that new people are being hired at a higher salary level than you when you have been doing a competent job for five years.

These are just a few examples of the personal and social stressors that we experience in a work context.

Let's look deeper into the stress reaction and how it can manifest in both the three Fs and what we call the three As.

When we get stressed or perceive threat, we may 'fight' and externalise our stress reaction, or choose 'flight' and internalise our stress reaction, or 'freeze' by procrastinating and shutting down.

All of these reactions will show up in our body, our thoughts, our feelings and emotions, and in our behaviours.

Fight Mode ('Anger')

When we react with fight, we externalise our reaction. We get angry, so we judge, we criticise and we attack others. We see them as wrong, so we blame and shame them.

Some of our reactions (out loud or to ourselves) might be:

- *You shouldn't have done that!*
- *You are wrong!*
- *How dare you do this to me!*
- *I will make you pay for this!*
- *Why do I have to work with such idiots?*
- *Why do people keep making mistakes?*
- *Why do people not do things properly and my way?*
- *Why are you doing this to me?*

Many people have the fight reaction as their normal stress reaction. For example, when feeling under pressure, someone may attack and blame before asking questions calmly to figure out what has happened.

Another example of this 'fight' reaction is when I saw a young child fall in a playground, and the adult's angry reaction was 'what did you do that for, you idiot'. I don't think that this is the reaction of an uncaring and callous person, but of someone who doesn't know how to control their stress reaction to the situation of a child hurting themselves.

Flight Mode ('Anxiety')

When we do the flight/flee reaction, we internalise our reaction. We get anxious, so we judge, criticise and attack ourselves. We see ourselves as wrong, so we blame and shame ourselves.

Some of our reactions (out loud or to ourselves) might be:

- *Why am I such an idiot?*
- *Why do I keep making mistakes?*
- *How could I have screwed up so badly?*
- *My life is such a mess.*
- *I will never amount to anything.*
- *Other people are always better than me.*
- *I am not good enough!*
- *I am not worthy!*
- *Why is this happening to me?*
- *I hate this job.*
- *I hate this traffic.*
- *Everything is out of control!*
- *The world is going to hell in a handbasket!*
- *Why do people keep picking on me?*
- *Why do I always have the bad luck?*
- *Why can't I get my life together?*
- *Everything is just so hard!*
- *I do not know how long I can keep going like this!*

Many people have this response as their normal stress reaction, particularly when experiencing significant stress and pressure that is loaded on top of existing stress.

For example, if a manager has an externalising stress reaction style, then under increasing amounts of pressure and stress, their tendency will be to get frustrated and angry, and hence attack others, blame others and find fault. This is an example of why bullying and harassment can exist in high stress workplaces, especially when individuals are experiencing high stress loads in their personal lives, which can get triggered in the work environment.

On the other hand, if a manager has an internalising reaction style, under pressure they may become extra anxious and start shaming themselves for everything causing that pressure. They might also become avoidant, and procrastinate in making decisions, or not dealing with a team member's bad behaviour – to the detriment of the whole team (or company!).

Both stress reactions come with their own challenges and affect workplace dynamics and activities differently, but both can also lead to the same end: a decline in workplace safety and well-being.

Freeze Mode ('Avoidance')

We do the freeze stress reaction when we avoid, procrastinate or numb out. Instead of reacting, we simply don't; we distract and deflect. For example, we may lean into substance abuse or distracting behaviours (like doom-scrolling, shopping, gambling, porn, gaming, excessive cleaning, excessive exercising, excessive working, etc.) to procrastinate and avoid the issue.

The important thing for us to be aware of is that when we ourselves or someone else is consistently blaming others, shaming themselves or repeatedly complaining, it could be indicative of significant mental and emotional stresses that we/they are dealing with.

It is very easy to be judgmental and make them feel wrong for being that way. But we need to be self-aware, empathetic and compassionate while also being mindful of our own mental and emotional health. If we are struggling, then we need to be looking after our own mental and emotional health.

If we see and hear that someone else is struggling, then ideally, if we can, we should connect and provide appropriate support. I will show you how to do this in Chapter 4.

However, one of our challenges as humans is that, when we are in our personal stress reaction, we think we are 'right'.

When we are **angry,** we are often convinced 'I am right'. By default, that means 'you are wrong' – 'you are making mistakes'; 'you are disagreeing with me'; 'you are trying to undermine my authority and make me look bad/weak'.

We are often convinced that our perspective/view is the only one, and we can't see counterpoints to it or dive into root causes.

The same thing happens when we are anxious – we believe we are right: 'I can't do this' or 'I will surely do it wrong'. Therefore, we have thoughts like 'I have screwed up'; 'I always make mistakes'; 'I am a loser'; 'People are always finding fault with me'; 'I will never be enough'.

And if your brain is in freeze mode, we don't know what to think – or we don't even want to think at all! I remember all too well as a teenager, the many times my mother would say to say to me, 'What did you do that for? What were you thinking?' And I can remember being so stressed and perplexed that I had no idea why I just did what I did!

These personal stress reactions are ingrained from our very early days and years. They take a lot of self-awareness work to change them and rise above them. If your personal stress reactions are negatively impacting your relationships, your work or your life, then you might want to begin the healing journey through self-help or professional help.

The Big Causes of Stress at Work and in Life

Research studies by the World Health Organization, the National Institute for Occupational Safety and Health, and the American Psychological Association have identified the major causes of stress at work and in life. The graphic below outlines the five biggest stressors for both workplace environments and generally in life. Any stressor in one area can in turn influence and exacerbate others.

THE 5 BIGGEST WORKPLACE STRESSORS AND THE 5 BIGGEST LIFE STRESSORS THAT IMPACT THE MENTAL HEALTH OF PEOPLE AT WORK

WORKPLACE STRESSORS

- **Workload:** Heavy workloads and deadlines can cause employees to feel overwhelmed and stressed.
- **Interpersonal conflict:** Conflicts with coworkers or superiors can lead to tension and anxiety.
- **Job insecurity:** Fear of losing one's job or being laid off can cause significant stress.
- **Lack of control:** Feeling powerless or unable to make decisions can lead to stress and frustration.
- **Poor work-life balance:** Difficulty balancing work and personal responsibilities can cause stress and burnout.

LIFE STRESSORS

- **Financial problems:** Struggling with debt, financial insecurity, or unemployment can cause significant stress.
- **Relationship issues:** Problems with romantic partners, family members, or friends can cause anxiety and depression.
- **Health problems:** Serious illnesses, chronic conditions, or injuries can have a significant impact on mental health.
- **Major life changes:** Significant life changes, such as marriage, divorce, death of someone close, moving, or the birth of a child, can be stressful.
- **Traumatic events:** Experiencing or witnessing a traumatic event, such as violence or natural disaster, can have a significant impact on mental health

What is the Difference Between Stress and Burnout?

While stress and burnout are related concepts, there are some important distinctions between the two.

Stress is a normal and often necessary response to challenges and demands in life. It is a physiological and psychological response to a perceived threat or challenge, and it can be triggered by a variety of factors, such as work pressure, financial difficulties or relationship problems. When it is more of a temporary challenge, stress can even sometimes be harnessed to have positive effects on performance, but either way, it can be managed through a variety of coping strategies.

Burnout, on the other hand, is a chronic state of physical, emotional and mental exhaustion that is caused by prolonged exposure to high levels of stress, particularly in the workplace. Burnout is characterised by feelings of cynicism, detachment and a reduced sense of accomplishment, and it can have serious consequences for an individual's health and well-being.

While stress can be managed, burnout requires a more comprehensive approach that addresses the underlying causes of the condition.

The increasing rates of burnout

Burnout rates have been increasing in OECD developed countries:

- A survey conducted by the Mental Health Foundation in the United Kingdom in 2018 found that nearly three-quarters of UK adults had felt overwhelmed or unable to cope at some point in the past year due to stress. The survey also found that 32% of respondents had experienced suicidal thoughts or feelings because of stress.

- A study published in the Lancet Public Health in 2019 analysed data from the General Social Survey in the United States and found that rates of burnout among American adults had increased by almost 30% between 2011 and 2018. The study also found that burnout rates were highest among individuals who were unmarried, working in healthcare or social services, and had lower incomes.

- Another study conducted by the Health and Safety Executive in the United Kingdom found that work-related stress, anxiety, and depression accounted for 44% of all work-related ill health and 54% of all working days lost due to ill health in 2018 and 2019.

So, what can we do?

Solving the problem of burnout in and/or from the workplace definitely has its complexities, but three key evidence-based best practice themes include:

1. Promoting a healthy work-life balance;
2. Cultivating a positive work environment; and
3. Providing support and resources for employees to manage stress and maintain their well-being.

The Negative Impacts of the Media, Social Media and Advertising on our Mental and Emotional Health

There has been increasing research to investigate the negative impacts that exposure to media, social media and advertising can have on mental health. Some key potential impacts include:

1. **Body image and self-esteem:** Advertising often promotes unrealistic beauty standards, which can lead to body dissatisfaction and negative self-image. Social media can also exacerbate these issues by creating a constant

stream of images and messages that emphasise appearance and social status.

2. **Anxiety and depression:** Social media use has been linked to increased rates of anxiety, depression and loneliness. This correlation may be in part due to the pressure to present a perfect life online as well as the constant comparisons and fear of missing out that social media can foster.

3. **Addiction and distraction:** Excessive social media use can lead to addiction and distraction, which in turn interferes with productivity and relationships.

4. **Sleep disturbance:** The blue light emitted by screens can interfere with sleep, which can lead to fatigue and other negative health outcomes.

5. **Desensitisation to violence:** Exposure to violent media can lead to desensitisation, which can in turn change how individuals process or perceive violence and make it more difficult to empathise with victims of violence.

While not all media, social media and advertising have negative effects on our mental health – and not everyone will be affected in the same way – specialists encourage being mindful of our media use and taking steps to limit exposure to negative content when possible. This intentionality may include setting boundaries around social media use, seeking out positive and uplifting media content, and practicing self-care and stress-management techniques.

Being aware of A.C.E.s. – Adverse Childhood Experiences

Author's note: This information is not meant to be diagnostic, but indicative. Please consult a licensed healthcare professional if you might be concerned about yourself or someone else. Please also remember that just because someone had or is experiencing these adverse experiences doesn't mean they will definitely experience mental illness or injury.

We will finish this chapter by touching on the complex topic of adverse childhood experiences and how these may contribute to mental illness or injury.

Adverse Childhood Experiences (ACEs) refer to a range of traumatic experiences that can occur during childhood, such as abuse (physical, sexual or emotional), neglect or exposure to violence or substance abuse within the home. Research has shown that exposure to ACEs can have significant negative impacts on adolescent and adult mental health and physical health.

There have been several studies that have found that individuals who experienced ACEs are at greater risk of developing mental health problems, such as depression, anxiety and post-traumatic stress disorder (PTSD) in adulthood.

For example, a study published in the American Journal of Preventive Medicine in 2019 found that individuals who reported four or more ACEs were more than twice as likely to experience depression and more than three times as likely to experience anxiety compared to those who reported no ACEs.

Exposure to ACEs has also been linked to a range of negative health outcomes, including chronic health conditions, substance abuse and suicide. For example, a study published in the Journal of the American Medical Association in 2019 found that individuals who reported ACEs were at greater risk of attempting suicide and dying by suicide.

The impact of ACEs on adult mental health is thought to be due in part to changes in brain development and functioning that occur in response to chronic stress and trauma. ACEs can also have lasting effects on an individual's social and emotional development, making it more difficult to form healthy relationships and cope with stressors later in life.

In terms of how many people are impacted by ACEs, it's hard to say.

Many research studies indicate that a significant proportion of the population has been exposed to ACEs. A seminal study by the Center for Disease Control and Prevention (CDC) and Kaiser Permanente, which surveyed over 17,000 adults in the United States in the 1990s, found that nearly two-thirds of participants reported experiencing at least one ACE, and more than one in five reported experiencing three or more ACEs.

Since the publication of the original ACEs study, numerous studies have replicated these findings in different populations and countries. For example, a study conducted in Canada in 2018 found that 64% of participants reported experiencing at least one ACE, and 13% reported experiencing four or more ACEs. Another study conducted in the United Kingdom in 2021 found that 70% of participants reported experiencing at least one ACE, and 9% reported experiencing four or more ACEs.

ACEs are not limited to specific populations or demographic groups; they are experienced across socioeconomic, racial and ethnic groups. However, some studies have found that certain groups, such as those from low-income backgrounds and those from marginalised communities, are more likely to experience multiple ACEs.

Overall, the research suggests that ACEs are a common experience among the population, and they can have significant negative impacts on adult mental health and well-being. Addressing ACEs through prevention and early intervention, investigating the root causes of childhood trauma, and providing support and resources for those who have experienced ACEs may help to mitigate these negative impacts and outcomes.

A reminder: The information provided here is for educational purposes only and is not intended as a substitute for professional clinical diagnosis or treatment. This material is not intended to be used for self-diagnosis or to replace the advice of a qualified healthcare professional. If you are experiencing mental health concerns, or this material is raising some uncomfortable emotions or thoughts, please seek the guidance of a licensed mental health provider. You can also seek immediate appropriate support via a family member, friend or colleague, or a helpline like Beyond Blue (on 1300 22 4636), Lifeline (on 13 11 14) or your Employee Assistance Provider.

The purpose of this chapter was to provide a broad understanding of mental health awareness. Personally, I think that it is critically important that all leaders and managers have this basic understanding and awareness for two reasons:

1. I gnorance is not bliss in this instance. There are work, health and safety (WHS) regulations that make such awareness and related support a legal responsibility for leaders and managers to make their workplaces psychosocially safe.

2. Rather than having a compliance mindset, it can be incredibly rewarding to create a workplace that truly cares about and values the humans who do the work!

CHAPTER 3

THE CHALLENGES – IN HAVING THE CONVERSATION

"The only way to change the world is to change yourself."

– Nelson Mandela

"Mental health is not a taboo subject. It's something that affects us all, and we need to talk about it."

– Unknown

PEOPLE NEED HELP SO WHAT CAN WE DO?

Now that you're feeling more aware of mental health in general, how do you bring it up and have the conversation?

It is not a simple thing to do.

You may already be quite familiar with the 'RUOK?' or 'Are You Okay?' campaign. It is a fantastic program to create awareness of mental health, but it is not always the easiest question to ask. And what do you do if they say, 'No, I'm not OK!' or something similar. Many people are reluctant to ask the question in the first place because of this very real uncertainty.

Sometimes the 'are you okay?' question may not be the best question to ask, either.

Because, in some instances, if you haven't built the relationship and trust, then some people might be insulted or put off by the question.

We are going to explore how you safely approach and ask someone how they are.

This is done by noticing the signs, knowing how to initiate the conversation, knowing how to listen, knowing how to help the person create self-awareness for their situation, and guiding them to a range of resources that could support them through whatever they are going through.

First let's look at the barriers to these conversations, and then we will explore how to have the conversations themselves.

Why Don't Leaders, Managers, Team Members and People in General Have Conversations About Mental Health?

Is it a will issue? They don't care?

Or is it a skill issue? They don't know how?

The answer is that it is a combination of both!

Most people who are emotionally aware and mature really do care. However, many people do not have the skills to be able to approach, connect and have these conversations.

We covered earlier that talking about mental health is perceived by many people to be scary, because they feel afraid:

- Of saying the wrong thing.
- That they will make it worse.
- It will make the other person angry.
- Of not knowing how to handle it.
- They cannot solve the problem.
- That it is a waste of time, and the person would not take my advice anyway.
- If I asked the suicide question, it might put the idea into their head.

Managers are also reluctant to talk to their team members about mental health because they are often already incredibly busy, so they often fear being overburdened with the mental health challenges of their staff. They also often lack the confidence and the competence to have the conversations (especially since these conversations are not about 'solving a problem' in the traditional sense). This dynamic is very challenging for most managers because their fundamental identity and reason for existence is to solve problems and tell people what to do.

There are six key reasons why managers may be reluctant to talk about mental health with their team members:

1.Stigma
2. Lack of training
3. Fear of saying the wrong thing
4. Privacy/legal concerns
5. Time constraints
6. Lack of resources

WHY MANAGERS MAY BE RELUCTANT TO TALK ABOUT MENTAL HEALTH WITH THEIR TEAM MEMBERS

1

STIGMA
Despite growing awareness and understanding of mental health issues, there is still a significant amount of stigma attached to mental illness. Many managers may feel uncomfortable discussing mental health with their team members due to concerns about how it will be perceived by others.

2

LACK OF TRAINING
Managers may not have received adequate training or education about mental health, which can make them feel unprepared to address these issues with their team members.

3

FEAR OF SAYING THE WRONG THING
Some managers may worry that they will say the wrong thing or make things worse if they try to discuss mental health with their team members.

4

PRIVACY CONCERNS
Managers may be hesitant to discuss mental health with their team members out of concern for their privacy and the confidentiality of their personal information.

5

TIME CONSTRAINTS
Many managers already have a lot on their plate, and may not feel like they have the time to address mental health concerns with their team members.

6

LACK OF RESOURCES
Some managers may feel that they don't have the resources or support they need to address mental health issues in the workplace, such as access to mental health professionals or employee assistance programs

What Makes a Leader/Manager More Likely or Less Likely to Provide Support?

Tony Jorm and Alyssia Rosetto in their research on help-giving towards people with a mental health problem [2015] identified the following reasons why some people may be more and less likely to provide mental health support.

The Motivators: What makes leaders/managers MORE likely to provide support?

1. A sense of care and compassion
2. Ability to recognise signs and symptoms
3. Feeling they have the knowledge & skills
4. Emotional resources
5. Closeness of the relationship
6. Level of danger

The Barriers: What makes leaders/managers LESS likely to provide support?

1. Feeling it is not their "place"
2. Fear of rejection
3. Fear of overreliance
4. Fear of being overburdened
5. Lack of confidence
6. Perceptions of person's motivation to change
7. Perceptions of impact of helping on our lives
8. Perceptions of severity of symptoms

For example, a team member might be underperforming and struggling, and as a manager, colleague or friend, you connect in and have a conversation with them. We'll teach you how to approach these conversations in more depth in Chapter 4, but for now let's assume they are not travelling too well and there is a level of trust, so they open up to you and say: 'I am really feeling a lot of pressure and stress at work and at home, and I think I am suffering from anxiety.'

Now, if you do not know how to respond to their statement, it would be easy to be cynical and judgmental with your thoughts and body language. The judgmental and cynical part of you might say to yourself, 'Here they go, "pulling the mental health card"' and hence you would be be less likely to provide support.

Instead, being able to withhold judgement and respond with a skilled, compassionate response like 'That must be very difficult for you' will create a much more supportive space. You could also pause and allow yourself and the other person to feel the empathy you are giving to them. If you have not had this type of interaction before, it will feel uncomfortable and emotionally stressful for you at first. That is okay – stay with your empathetic and compassionate feelings.

The conversation might then continue with something like:

> *'Have you got support and resources to help you with what you are experiencing?'*

> *'No, I've talked to my friends, I have been to Google and I have definitely got anxiety.'*

> *'Just so I understand, have you seen your doctor to talk about what you are experiencing?'*

This is exactly how you would respond in the same situation if a team member was maybe experiencing pains in their stomach, and you gently asked, *'Have you seen your doctor about these pains?'*

Side Note: At this point many managers (and people in general) would like the answers to questions such as:

> *How do I deal with a situation in which someone is self-diagnosing?*

When does a couple of days or a week off become a diagnosable mental illness?

When do the normal pressures and stresses of a job or relationships or life become a concern for someone's mental health?

Remember our mantra from earlier: if **symptoms persist, please see your healthcare professional.** It is not up to us to play doctor or therapist.

Chapter 4 will prepare you to handle this type of situation in an effective way. We will also cover how to approach a situation where the person is resistant and doesn't want help.

Self-care for the Leader/Manager/Team Leader

Self-care is essential for managers dealing with work pressures and the mental health challenges of their team members. Research has shown that taking care of your physical and mental health is crucial for your overall well-being, and this is particularly true for managers who face high levels of stress and responsibility.

It is vital that managers reach out for support when they feel that they need it. There is no weakness in this – in fact, it is a strong, intelligent thing to do!

What I have found from my own experience is that when I have discussions with professionals to look after my self-care, I get smarter, stronger and more skilful in handling complex situations.

I provide you with many self-care strategies in Chapter 5.

Studies have found that managers who prioritise self-care are more likely to experience greater job satisfaction, better work-life balance and improved mental health. They are also better equipped to support their team members' mental health needs and create a positive and supportive work environment.

Moreover, the managers who practise self-care are better able to manage stress, handle conflicts, and make sound decisions. This dynamic, in turn, can lead to increased productivity and better performance among team members.

Overall, the research suggests that self-care is an essential aspect of effective management, particularly in today's fast-paced and high-pressure work environments. By prioritising self-care, managers can not only take care of their own well-being, but also support their team members' mental health needs and create a positive and productive work environment.

Why is Talking About Feelings & Emotions Considered to be a Sign of Weakness?

I have admittedly had this point of view in the past. It is a pervasive view held by many people. It exists in workplaces and families and across many cultures.

There are many complex reasons why we don't want to talk about our vulnerable feelings. Some examples might be 'I'm the provider, the protector, and I am supposed to be strong' – and there are hundreds more.

However, one of the big challenges that I have experienced from my own life, and from talking with others, is the perception and the experience that to talk about our feelings is UNSAFE. In other words, we will get hurt – we will be judged, criticised, ridiculed, ostracised and demoted.

This line of thinking happens – a lot. Here is a way of thinking about solving this problem from a different perspective.

As humans we are highly emotionally tuned to others – particularly those people who are close to us. What happens when we are talking with someone experiencing emotional pain is that we will feel that person's pain in our own bodies and minds. Most people are not conscious of feeling this pain, and so unconsciously, it will trigger their personal stress reaction.

Most people will therefore react with fight (*'Come on mate, you'll get over it – what are you complaining about? Suck it up!'*) or flight (*'What's the matter with you? Why are you feeling like that – who do you think you are, princess?'*). Or, they're freeze and deflect.

These reactions – judgement, criticism, ridicule, sarcasm or avoidance – are very hurtful, so why would a person open up? It feels UNSAFE!

But imagine if the person receiving the information is self-aware. They will notice their stress reaction, stop the reaction and respond with empathy, compassion and kindness. Then the space to share could be an emotionally welcoming and safe one, where we could help that person feel safe and develop their own awareness of their situation and what they need. (Remember: no telling them what to do or trying to 'solve' their 'problem'!)

My observation and personal experience is that we don't create these safe environments for a person to talk about how they are feeling, which can exacerbate any ideas of perceived 'weakness' in the act of opening up. Until I did Lifeline training, I didn't know how to talk about my own feelings of being uncertain and vulnerable. Instead, I kept those feelings to myself – because I never felt safe to talk about them.

However, what I learnt from Lifeline is that our self-care is extremely important, and what Lifeline do is that they very strongly encourage us to look after our self-care by having debrief discussions and supervision sessions so that we can talk about any distressed feelings and not keep them suppressed inside our minds and bodies.
Otherwise, the suppression leads to depression and aggression.

If we all change as individuals and as a culture – and stop blaming, shaming or avoiding someone when they express their vulnerabilities and challenges – and we access our own strength of character to be empathetic and compassionate, environments everywhere would be better places. My perspective is that when these feelings are shared, listened to and validated in a safe context, they make us emotionally and mentally stronger.

As I have been saying, the brain is just another body part. When we want to get physically stronger, we might go to the gym or work with a trainer. The same is true for mental strength: we get stronger emotionally by lifting the difficult 'weights' of life experiences, with ourselves, with others and with trained professionals.

As Mark Curry shares:

'Another simple point that I would add from my own experience is that, despite the internal barriers to be overcome in revealing one's personal/emotional issues to others, **the act of sharing** these feelings/experiences with another human being – **who is prepared to listen** to them in good faith and without judgement – almost always results in an immediate sense of some relief, some reduction of the burden you have been carrying around on your own.

I guess this is something to do with the interconnectedness of all humans and our strong need for this connection – no one is an island, etc.

I think this simple act of sharing is valuable and is also the underlying basis for the effectiveness of Lifeline, Counselling and Clinical Psychology.'

As a succinct summary for this chapter, I particularly like this quote from Adam Grant, Organisational Psychologist, Author and Professor at the Wharton School of the University of Pennsylvania:

> *'In toxic cultures, being a workaholic is normalised, and sacrificing sleep is glorified, and the best way to get ahead is to burn out. Whereas in healthy cultures, quality of life is expected, and having a life is celebrated. You are encouraged to put your well-being above your work.'*

THE SKILLS – FOR S.A.F.E CONVERSATIONS

"Mental health is not a luxury, it's a necessity. Without it, we cannot be our best selves."

– Joyce Meyer

"The greatest discovery of my generation is that a human being can alter his life by altering his attitudes of mind."

– William James

In this chapter we are now going to dive into understanding the mental health conversation skills for leaders, managers and team members in a work context. However, these skills will also be relevant in non-work contexts with partners, family and friends.

This **S.A.F.E.** framework – which involves **S**elf-awareness and awareness of others, **A**cknowledging and asking, **F**ocusing on listening, and **E**mpowering – is equally applicable whether you are in a leadership role or in a non-leadership role, because it is about the ability to have conversations with others that are S.A.F.E – ones that are done with empathy and care for the other person.

The Distinction Between Task- or Performance-Focused Conversations and Person-Centred Conversations

Firstly, we need to recognise the distinction between task/ performance-focused conversations and person-centred conversations.

If you are a boss, manager or team leader, then your job is about getting things done through people. I am going to assume that because you are in your role, that you are capable – you know what tasks must be done and what outcomes must be achieved.

You have task-based, performance-focused conversations all the time. Some examples are listed in the table below.

THE TASK-FOCUSED CONVERSATIONS THAT MANAGERS MIGHT HAVE WITH THEIR TEAM MEMBERS

SETTING GOALS AND EXPECTATIONS
Managers might have conversations with their team members to discuss and clarify the goals and expectations for a project or task.

1

2

PROVIDING FEEDBACK
Managers might have conversations with team members to provide feedback on their work, both positive and constructive, and to help them improve their performance.

DELEGATING TASKS
Managers might have conversations with team members to delegate specific tasks and responsibilities, ensuring that the workload is distributed effectively.

3

4

CHECKING PROGRESS
Managers might have conversations with team members to check on the progress of a project or task, to ensure that everything is on track and to address any issues that arise.

PROBLEM-SOLVING
Managers might have conversations with team members to brainstorm solutions to problems or challenges that arise during a project or task.

5

6

PERFORMANCE EVALUATION
Managers might have conversations with team members to evaluate their performance, set goals for improvement, and plan for professional development.

Often those conversations will be fast. You are creating accountability with the other person because the job needs to be done, and the outcomes need to be achieved.

Person-centered conversations are the conversations that we are going to learn to do now. They are a very different type of conversation that involves trust on a different level, because the focus is on someone rather than something.

These conversations are ones in which you are connecting with the other person, both mentally and emotionally. They are about enabling the other person to experience feeling heard, validated and listened to. Your role is guiding that person to come to their own self-awareness and empowering them to make appropriate decisions in order to look after themselves. It's not about assigning or dictating an expectation, solution or outcome.

Person-centred conversations require a lot of skill.

- You need to be self-aware.
- You need to create a S.A.F.E space.
- You need to slow down and be comfortable with silence.
- You need to connect with your own feelings.
- You need to notice the feelings of the other person and be able to connect with them at that level as well.
- You need to listen and acknowledge.
- You need to empower the other person to choose their own next steps.

To develop these skills, this chapter will teach you:

1. How to initiate the conversation
2. How to ask the right questions
3. How to listen effectively
4. How to respond appropriately with the right guidance

S.A.F.E conversations are **NOT** about:

1. Being someone's therapist.
2. Being someone's best buddy or confidante.
3. Making excuses for someone's poor performance.
4. Making excuses for someone's disruptive behaviour or language.

S.A.F.E conversations are about making these conversations safe for yourself and for the other person. This is a conversation in which your primary focus is on connecting with the other person and really listening.

Your manager-brain or problem-solving brain will be focused on telling them what to do and solving their problem. However, you cannot go there.

This conversation is about connecting with a person where they are, in an appropriate and authentic way that is aligned to your own style.

Your aim is to connect, listen and empower the person to identify resources and support that would be most appropriate to them. These skills are usable anywhere, in any context – in an office, factory, virtual workplace and at home.

Levels of S.A.F.E. Conversations

There are three levels of S.A.F.E conversations that depend on the specific situation of the other person.

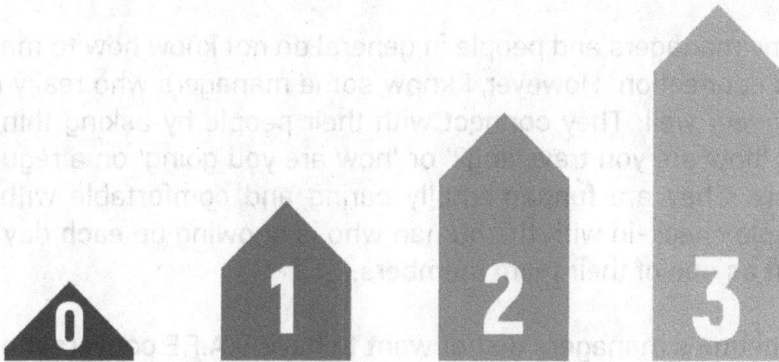

LEVEL 0	LEVEL 1	LEVEL 2	LEVEL 3
not seeing any signs	seeing/hearing the signs that someone may be struggling	seeing/hearing significant signs that indicate the person is in a more difficult situation and recognising how to escalate to professional resources	crisis signs such as the person is having suicidal thoughts, engaging in self-harm (non-suicidal self-injury), severe panic attacks, severe psychosis

Level 0: You are not seeing or hearing any signs or symptoms of mental health difficulties. S.A.F.E conversations at this level enable you to be proactive and connect with another person purely based on them as a person, separate from the tasks that they do or the performance that is expected of them.

Some managers and people in general do not know how to make this connection. However, I know some managers who really do this very well. They connect with their people by asking things like 'how are you travelling?' or 'how are you going' on a regular basis. They are fundamentally caring and comfortable with a simple check-in with the human who is showing up each day or shift as one of their team members.

Sometimes managers do not want to have S.A.F.E conversations at this level because they are concerned about rocking the boat – they do not want to get too personal, and so therefore, they stay very task focused.

But if the personal stuff does come up, **it is not your problem to solve.**

This person is a fully functioning human who has the capacity to solve their own problems. What they need is to feel heard, listened to and validated as a human being. They need the guidance and assistance to access their own resources or professional resources, as appropriate. S.A.F.E conversations help you do that.

Level 1: You are seeing or hearing mild signs or symptoms that someone is struggling. We have covered these signs earlier. It will be one or more of the three Fs of Fight/Flight/Freeze that is showing up as one or more of the three As of Anger/Anxiety/Avoidance. You will be seeing and hearing some blaming, shaming, complaining and/or avoiding.

Level 2: You are seeing or hearing significant signs that indicate the person is in a more difficult and stressful situation. Here is when you need to be especially aware in recognising how and when to escalate to professional resources.

MILD VS SIGNIFICANT
WHAT'S THE DIFFERENCE?

- Mental health challenges and difficulties can vary in severity, and the signs and symptoms can differ depending on the specific condition and individual. However, there are some general differences between mild and significant mental health challenges.

- Someone experiencing mild mental health challenges may have symptoms that are not severe enough to significantly impact their daily life or ability to function. They may experience occasional feelings of sadness, worry, or stress, but these feelings do not persist for an extended period or cause significant impairment in their daily activities. Other symptoms may include changes in sleep patterns, appetite, or energy levels.

- On the other hand, someone experiencing significant mental health challenges may have symptoms that significantly impact their daily life and ability to function. They may experience persistent feelings of sadness, anxiety, or irritability that interfere with their ability to work, socialize, or take care of themselves. They may also experience changes in their sleep patterns, appetite, or energy levels, as well as physical symptoms such as headaches or stomach problems.

- In more severe cases, individuals may experience hallucinations or delusions, have difficulty distinguishing reality from fantasy, or engage in self-harm or suicidal behaviors.

- It's important to note that mental health challenges exist on a continuum, and there is no clear line between mild and significant symptoms. What may be mild for one individual could be significant for another. It's essential to seek professional help if you or someone you know is experiencing mental health challenges, that you have increasing concerns about, regardless of the severity of the symptoms.

Level 3: The person is in crisis. They are possibly having suicidal thoughts or engaging in self-harm (non-suicidal self-injury), or they might be experiencing severe panic attacks or severe psychosis. We provide specific guidance for these situations in Chapter 6.

Mental Health First Aid accredited training or an equivalent certificate is required for you to have the skills and knowledge to able to handle crisis situations. If you are interested in such training, please see the information in Chapter 7.

Author's note:

In every level of these conversations, please remember that the information provided here is for educational purposes only and is not intended as a substitute for professional clinical diagnosis or treatment. If you or someone you know is experiencing mental health concerns, please seek the guidance of a licensed healthcare provider.

The Four Skills of S.A.F.E Conversations

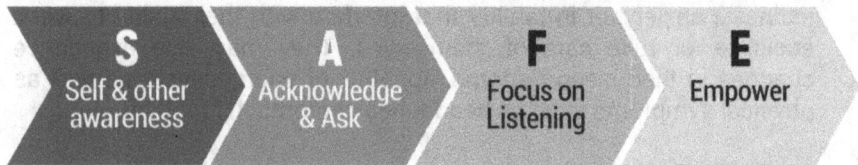

S	A	F	E
Self & other awareness	Acknowledge & Ask	Focus on Listening	Empower

TASK-FOCUSED CONVERSATIONS

PERSON-CENTRED CONVERSATIONS

Skill 1 ('S'): Self-awareness and other awareness

The first step with these conversations is to be self-aware. You are connecting with another human to build trust, rapport and empathy. It is important that you are in the 'empathy mindset' of being genuine and nonjudgmental. I will elaborate on that shortly.

If you are not familiar with these types of conversations it will feel 'a bit icky' (the 'technical' term for uncomfortable!).

It will often trigger your personal stress reaction and you will either:

- **Fight:** externalise and blame the other person (*'I am wasting my time; they do not want to change, or can't change, and they won't want me sticking my nose into their personal stuff'*)
- **Flight:** internalise and shame yourself (*'I am sure they won't like me for doing this, and I am sure I will mess it up – what if they get angry at me?'*)
- **Freeze:** avoid the conversation until it gets worse.

You will need practice and persistence. You will need to develop your emotional skills and emotional awareness.

Being self-aware means having a deep understanding of your own emotions, thoughts and behaviours. It involves being able to recognise your strengths and weaknesses, your values and beliefs, and how you react to different situations.

Self-awareness is a critical skill for managers and for your personal and professional development, as it enables you to make better decisions, manage your emotions effectively and build stronger relationships with others.

You can develop your self-awareness by:

- Reflecting on your experiences.

- Seeking feedback.
- Practicing mindfulness.
- Keeping a journal.

An example of self-awareness on the job is a manager who can recognise when they are feeling overwhelmed or stressed and take steps to manage their emotions effectively, such as taking a break or delegating tasks. They may also be able to identify their own biases and limitations, and work to overcome these to build stronger relationships with their team members.

THE S.A.F.E CONVERSATION SKILLS

S. Self & other awareness

1 Be self-aware to connect & build trust, rapport and empathy

2 Be genuine and non-judgemental

3 Consider the other person and their situation

Prepare for the conversation-are you in the right frame of mind?

Do you have the time?

Consider the other person and their situation where will you have the conversation?

How will you open the conversation and make a genuine connection?

Hi Emily/Tom, how are things going for you ....?

How are you travelling .....?

Preparing for the conversation means asking yourself these questions:

- Are you in the right frame of mind?
- Do you have the time?
- Is this an appropriate time for you and for them?
- Consider the other person – where will you have the conversation? It is often a good practice to 'walk and talk', even grab a coffee, to ease some potential pressure!
- How will you start the dialogue and make a genuine connection?

If you are not in a good place – if you are under pressure or if you are frustrated, angry or anxious – do not have the conversation. It is not an appropriate time.

These conversations are NOT supposed to be big, deep and meaningful sessions. We are not talking about 30 minutes or more – maybe five minutes. Sometimes it might need a little extra time – depending on the person's situation. But you will still need to have the appropriate time and headspace.

Here are examples, which you can tailor to your own language and approach.

- *Hi _____, how are things going for you?*
- *How are you travelling?*
- *Would you like to...?*
- *Let's go grab a coffee.*
- *Let's have a quick chat.*
- *Let's go for a walk.*
- *Do you have time for a..?*

EMPATHY VS SYMPATHY

Empathy is about them ['em]

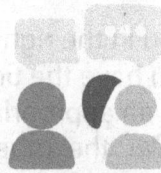

Sympathy is about self

S.A.F.E conversations are empathy conversations. Empathy is all about 'them'. It is about connecting with what the other person is feeling. It is the idea of putting ourselves into the other person's shoes.

Sympathy has a focus on 'self'.

Empathy and sympathy are often used interchangeably, but they have distinct meanings. Empathy refers to the ability to understand and share the feelings of **another** person, whereas with sympathy, we focus on our **own** feelings about someone else's situation/misfortune.

In a mental health conversation context within a workplace, here are some examples:

Empathy:

1. 'It sounds like you are dealing with significant challenges outside of work. What support and resources do you have to help you through that?'
2. 'That must be very concerning for you with your mother's health getting worse. How are you feeling and what support are you getting?'

Sympathy:

1. 'I'm so sorry that you're struggling with your mental health. I hope things get better for you soon.'
2. 'It breaks my heart to hear what you're going through. Let me know if there's anything I can do to help.'

WHY IS EMPATHY MORE EFFECTIVE THEN SYMPATHY

The research into the effectiveness of Empathy compared to Sympathy in mental health conversations has highlighted the following reasons:

- **CONNECTION:** Empathy allows the person to feel understood and validated, which can help them feel less alone and more connected to others.

- **PROBLEM-SOLVING:** Empathy encourages problem-solving, as the person providing empathy is better equipped to understand the situation and offer solutions. In contrast, sympathy tends to focus more on comforting the person, often by telling them what to do, or just feeling sorry for the person without necessarily offering solutions.

- **SELF-EFFICACY:** Empathy can increase the person's self-efficacy and motivation to make changes, as they feel that they have support and understanding from others. Sympathy may unintentionally reinforce feelings of helplessness and powerlessness.

- **TRUST:** Empathy builds trust between the two people, as the person receiving empathy feels that they can trust the person providing empathy to understand and support them. Sympathy can sometimes come across as insincere or superficial or arrogant, which can erode trust.

You don't connect with another person emotionally by talking about yourself first.

We have all had the experience in which we might share something that is going on for us, and the other person responds by totally shifting the conversation to talking about themselves.

Some people think they are being helpful when they talk about themselves or their own experience, but that is the worst thing you can do when you begin a conversation with another person.

In the context of task/performance conversations, it can be useful to talk about yourself, your own experience, etc., to solve problems and get outcomes, because you have the specific experience.

But in S.A.F.E conversations, it is very important to hold back and not talk about ourselves prematurely. The reason is that we significantly disempower the person we are talking with when we make the conversation about us and not about them.

Let me explain. When we have a S.A.F.E conversation, we have an unspoken question of *'How can I help you?'* in our minds.

The thing that we must be so careful of is that, if our conscious or unconscious emphasis is on the 'I' or 'help', you will fundamentally be disempowering the other person. You might have the best intentions of trying to help or make things better, but this dynamic leaves the person feeling unsupported and unvalidated in being able to access their own resources to solve their own problems.

Consider these two examples I heard recently in my workshops:

A woman in her early 30s shared that when she has conversations with her mother, her mother is always trying to 'be helpful' and tell her what to do. She has to say to her mother, *'Hey mom, thank you for caring. I am 32 and I can look after myself.'*

Another person mentioned that they had told their manager, *'I am having a lot of challenges at home'* and the manager's immediate reaction was, *'I will change your shifts.'*

Think of the many times that other people have tried to be helpful and tell you what to do – what was your reaction? You either told them to p*%$# off or you just felt shamed and humiliated.

The emphasis of a S.A.F.E conversation is the 'You' in 'How can i [deliberate lower case] help **YOU**?' or 'What do YOU need?'

It is important for us to be totally focused on the other person in order to understand them, to have a sense of what they are feeling, to hear what is happening for them, and to understand what they have done so far and what resources they can access that will be helpful for them.

There is no 'I' here – initially. Yes, your guidance or personal experience may be valuable to share, but not early in the conversation.

I will show you shortly when it is more appropriate.

This communication skill is not easy, and it needs persistence and practice.

Most of us have not been taught to be present with another person and listen. We have grown up in families and work environments where we are constantly being told what to do, or where we are telling others what to do.

HOW WE EMPOWER OR DISEMPOWER THE OTHER PERSON

How can **I** help you
How can **I HELP** you
How can i help **YOU**

It is not a question — it is a MINDSET
It's not about **me**, it's all about **them!**

It's about *turning off* our manager
Brain and problem-solving brain

It is all about 'turning off' your manager brain and your problem-solving brain. We are not trying to solve their problems; we are not trying to tell them what to do. We are trying to help the other person become mindful and aware of what they need to access and what resources will work for them at this time.

Things to do to foster empathy:

1. Be self-aware and aware of others.
2. Be emotionally prepared.
3. Think about when is an appropriate time of day and place – for both of you.
4. Consider the most appropriate method to connect – phone or video call, Teams/Zoom, going for a walk, grabbing a coffee, texting sometimes, etc.
5. Start general in connecting to see how they are.
6. Be calm, patient and understanding – trust needs to be built slowly.
7. Really listen to their responses.
8. Pick up on cues, and then inquire further.
9. Ask open questions.

Things NOT to do:

1. Do not set the agenda at the start. In other words, if you are connecting in with somebody and having a conversation with them, particularly if it is the first time, you do not want to open with something like: 'Hey ____, I'd like to have a conversation with you *because I've noticed that you have been...'*

   What is that going to do? It will immediately put them on the defensive.

   It may seem to be the logical thing to do, particularly if you are a direct type of person and you want to get to the point. But do not make this about you. It is about them. So, you want to start general and use their name to increase connection.

   Now, if this is your second time connecting, and you can clearly see that they are not at their best, then gently referencing what you are noticing is an appropriate thing to do. But certainly not in the first conversation.

2. Do not force them to talk.
3. Do not make assumptions or generalisations.
4. Do not diagnose.
5. Do not problem-solve or give advice.
6. Do not worry too much about saying the wrong thing, because when we are coming from a place of care and consideration for the other person, they will feel it. They may push back. It may not be a good time. They may not feel like opening up about what is bothering them. But more than likely, they will leave the conversation noticing that you were trying to connect (and this is important).

Another way to think about the 'empathy mindset' is that it has three components.

EMPATHY

Cognitive Empathy Think	Emotional Empathy Feel	Compassionate Empathy Do

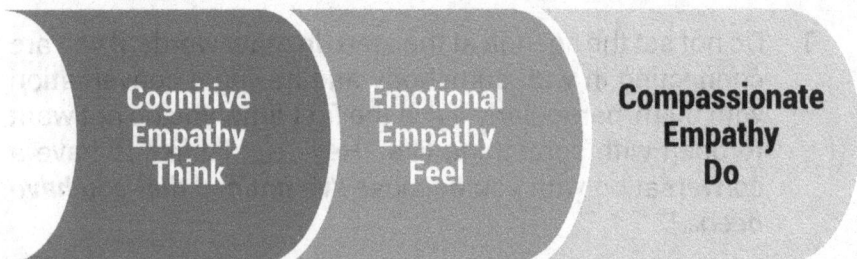

1. **Cognitive empathy** is when we think empathetically about a person's situation. For example, I watched a program recently that presented the experiences that refugees go through to leave their war-torn homeland and travel to and settle in another country. This situation is incredibly traumatising and difficult. I can imagine what it is like, but I haven't experienced it myself.

2. **Emotional empathy** is when we connect with the feelings that a person may be experiencing. Often, we do not know exactly how they are feeling, but it is very important to notice our own feelings. As humans, as socially connected

beings, we are highly sensitive to the emotions and feelings of others. We will feel the pain of people who are close to us.

The vital skill is to reflect these feelings back to the other person so that they feel heard, validated and listened to. It is so important that we have self-awareness of our feelings and do not consciously or unconsciously dump **our** feelings onto the other person by talking about ourselves or telling them what to do.

3. **Compassionate empathy** is when you engage in a S.A.F.E conversation. We must realise that these conversations will require emotional energy. You may well feel emotionally drained, or some degree of emotional disturbance in yourself, until you get quite practised at having S.A.F.E conversations. Therefore, it is critically important that you look after your own self-care. Notice your feelings and replenish your energy level. I will cover personal self-care strategies in Chapter 5, but briefly, a few quick tips: breathe; express gratitude; acknowledge positive thoughts and feelings; or do an aspect of your work that you enjoy. If you feel that you need additional support for yourself, I strongly encourage reaching out to your Employee Assistance Provider.

Skill 2 ('A'): Acknowledge and Ask

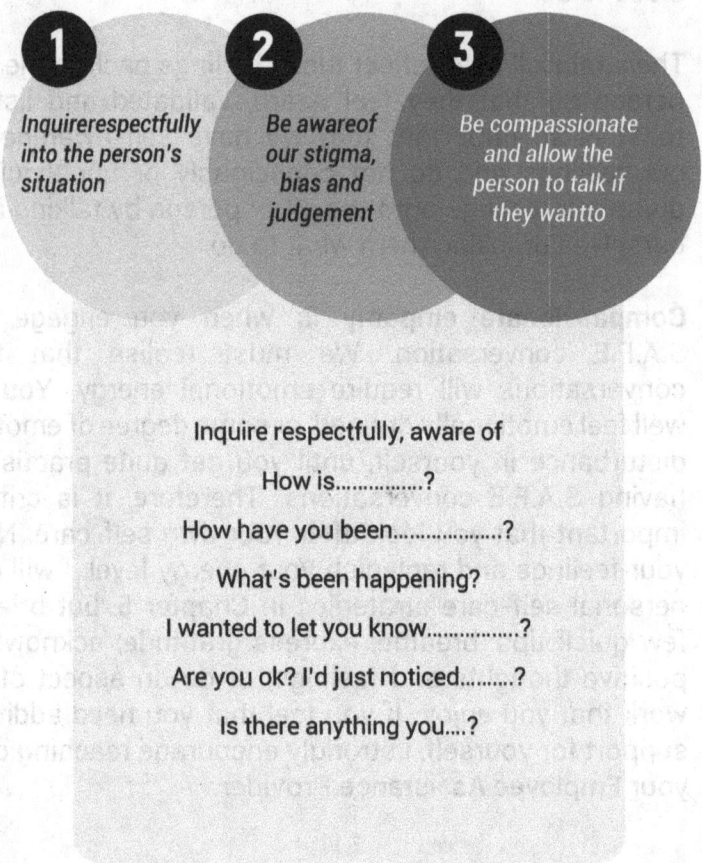

1

Inquire respectfully into the person's situation

2

Be aware of our stigma, bias and judgement

3

Be compassionate and allow the person to talk if they want to

Inquire respectfully, aware of

How is...............?

How have you been...................?

What's been happening?

I wanted to let you know................?

Are you ok? I'd just noticed..........?

Is there anything you....?

The second step of S.A.F.E conversations is to acknowledge and ask.

To acknowledge is to show or express recognition or realisation of something or someone. For example, to acknowledge an acquaintance by nodding.

In a S.A.F.E conversation, we are acknowledging the person's feelings and their situation. We inquire respectfully into their situation, allowing them to talk (if they want to) while being aware of any stigma or bias or judgment that we might be carrying. We are also asking (gently) general questions, listening closely and practising empathy and compassion.

We might ask questions like:

- *How is...?*
- *How have you been?*
- *What's been happening?*
- *I wanted to let you know...*
- *Are you okay?*
- *I just noticed... is there anything that you need? (Rather than 'What can I do for you?')*

Generally speaking, there are two types of questions we might ask.

1. Open questions will explore and guide. They will **open** the conversation. You use the 'w' and 'h' words – what, how, why, where, who and when. These words increase the probability that the question you ask will be open – the person is totally open to give whatever response they choose.
2. Closed questions will clarify and confirm. They will **close and narrow** the conversation rather than invite more response. Closed questions use the auxiliary verbs: - is, are, do, can, have, could.

It is important for us to be self-aware of our question styles, as they can guide the tone and effectiveness of the conversation.

A very good conversational structure is something like: open/open/closed or even open/open/open/closed. This approach will ensure that the person you are talking with will feel that the conversation is focused on them, and that they are not being interrogated.

Examples of interrogation type questions are:

- *Have you been getting enough sleep?*

- *Have you been staying off the alcohol?*
- *Don't you think that was a mistake?*
- *Wouldn't you agree that we should do it this way?*

Skill 3 ('F'): Focus on Listening

1

Use your listening skills to build empathy

2

Reflect what you are hearing - using their words

3

Acknowledge the challenges the person is experiencing

4

Be present with the person, and don't try to solve their problem

That must be.............

I can see that would be........

You seem...........

It sounds like you're feeling .....

Do you want to talk about it a bit more ......?

Let us face it. Listening is tough; it is hard to do!

If we take the word listen and rearrange the letters, we get silent.

If we listen well, where does that silence exist?

In our own heads!

Have you ever noticed that when having conversations with other people we are so often in our own heads, thinking about what they are saying, and waiting for them to take a breath, so that we can give them our perspective or opinion on what they are saying? That is not listening – that is hearing, judging and reacting!

Using our listening skills involves:

- reflecting what we are hearing.
- using their words to acknowledge the challenges that they are experiencing.
- being present and not trying to solve their problem.
- NOT solving, advising or trying to put a positive spin on someone's difficult situation.

Gently reflecting in a caring and authentic way is a particularly powerful skill. It's another way to build empathy and help the person feel heard and validated. This type of gentle reflection in a conversation might sound like:

- *That must be tough for you to be going through that.*
- *That must be really difficult to have had that relationship break up.*
- *It sounds like it is quite difficult for you at present with your parent being unwell, and the pressures and the challenges that must be creating for you.*
- *I can see that that would be ...*
- *What I am hearing is...*
- *It sounds like you're feeling...*
- *Do you want to talk about it a bit more?*

At this point, let me give you an example of a very poor communication skill —which a lot of people tend to do: toxic positivity.

The ABC (The Australian Broadcasting Commission) have a podcast called *All in The Mind,* which I was listening to a few months ago. This episode was about toxic positivity.

People will unknowingly practise toxic positivity when they try to be nice and helpful by trying to be positive and sometimes saying what ultimately come off as silly or inappropriate things.

An example that was shared in the program was a situation in which a woman who had one child had recently lost a second child in childbirth. One friend said to her, 'Well, at least you've got one.' This response is a classic example of toxic positivity.
What is far better in situations where someone is going through something difficult is to validate and reflect their feelings, not try to spin or smooth them over. These sorts of responses sound like:

- *That must be very painful for you.*
- *What support have you got to help you through that?*
- *What help are you receiving to support you through the very difficult feelings that you may be experiencing?*

Nobody wants, and nobody needs, another person trying to give them toxic, patronising solutions. The person is in pain, and what is most important is to sit with them in their pain – not because we are enabling it, but because we are sharing it and supporting them in not feeling alone in their pain.

To be an effective listener, you should practise these five skills:

1. Attention: Giving your full attention to the speaker and focusing on what they are saying. This involves avoiding distractions and putting aside any other thoughts or concerns.

2. Active Listening: Demonstrating that you are engaged and understanding the speaker by providing verbal and nonverbal feedback. This includes nodding, making appropriate facial expressions, and using phrases like 'I see' or 'Go on' to show that you are actively listening.
3. Empathy: Putting yourself in the speaker's shoes and trying to understand their perspective, emotions, and experiences. This involves being non-judgmental and avoiding making assumptions about what the speaker is thinking or feeling.
4. Curiosity: Asking questions to ensure that you have a clear understanding of what the speaker is saying. This can involve paraphrasing what they have said to ensure that you have correctly understood their meaning.
5. Patience: Allowing the speaker to take their time and express themselves fully without interrupting or rushing them. This can help the speaker feel heard and understood, and can also facilitate a more productive conversation.

THE LISTENING HIERARCHY

At What Level Do You Normally Listen?

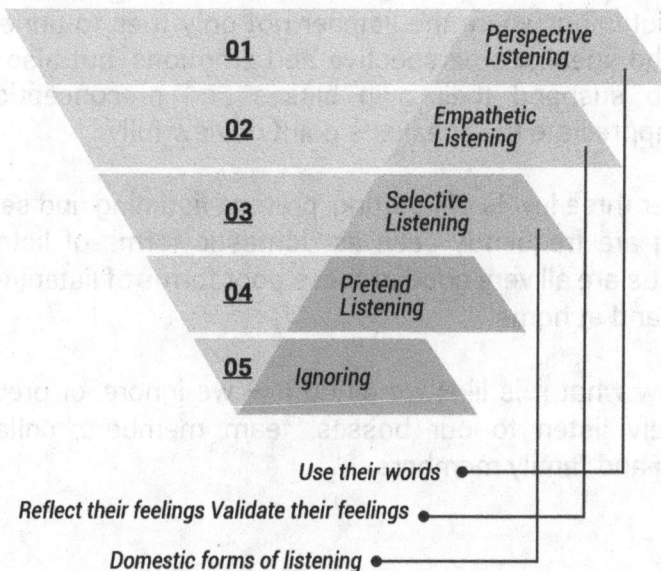

01	Perspective Listening
02	Empathetic Listening
03	Selective Listening
04	Pretend Listening
05	Ignoring

Use their words

Reflect their feelings Validate their feelings

Domestic forms of listening

In the Listening Hierarchy we can see five (5) levels of listening:

5. **Ignoring:** This is the lowest level of listening, where the listener is completely disengaged and not paying attention to the speaker.

4. **Pretend listening:** This is when the listener is physically present and appears to be listening, but is not actually paying attention to what the speaker is saying. Often, we choose to do something else at the same time.

3. **Selective listening:** This is when the listener only focuses on certain parts of the message that are of interest to them or that confirm their existing beliefs and ignores or discounts other parts of the message.

2. **Empathetic listening:** This involves paying attention to what the speaker is saying, and also actively trying to understand the speaker's feelings and emotions. The listener demonstrates empathy and a desire to understand the speaker's experience.

1. **Perspective listening:** This is the highest level of listening, where the listener not only tries to understand the speaker's perspective and emotions, but also works to suspend their own biases and preconceptions to appreciate the speaker's point of view fully.

The lower three levels of ignoring, pretend listening and selective listening are frequently seen as domestic forms of listening – most of us are all very good at these poor forms of listening, both at work and at home!

You know what it is like; we all do it – we ignore, or pretend or selectively listen to our bosses, team members, colleagues, partners and family members.

But when we listen **properly,** we will firstly listen for the feelings, and we will notice the feelings of the other person in our own bodies. We reflect those feelings in a caring and authentic way.

When we do this our partner, our children, our team member, our colleague or our friend will feel heard, validated and listened to.

The highest level of listening involves really hearing the words that the person uses and reflect these words as well.

If you use different words, you will break rapport, and their brain will interpret that you are not listening to them.

This is a subtle skill, but incredibly important.

Here is an example, have you ever been told - 'you are not listening to me'.

This will happen when we fall into the classic trap of being in our own heads, hearing the words, and responding with our interpretation of their words. **Our brain makes a judgement or diagnosis or has a solution, which we then communicate back.**

This is a big mistake and demonstrates poor skills in listening – a rookie error!

What your partner – or any anyone with whom you find yourself in a conversation – will hugely appreciate, is if you reflect their own words back to them to demonstrate you really are listening exactly to what they say, and you respond with empathy towards them and their situation. And, of course, NOT try to tell them what to do!

The 80-20 Rule in Listening

S.A.F.E conversations as person-centred conversations have an 80–20 airtime balance.

- 80% of the airtime is the person talking with you.
- 20% of the airtime will be your acknowledging, listening, reflecting feelings and asking questions, plus giving support and information when required.

In your task/performance conversations, the numbers are reversed – you do most of the talking.

Remember: To Listen = Silence inside your own head.

Again, this is easier said than done.

Cut yourself some slack if you have never done this before. Most people have not been trained in listening, and it is a skill that must be developed.

Initially, it is going to feel uncomfortable. You are going to be possibly annoyed, or anxious or uncertain about the application of these skills.

Just slow it down, have the conversation and enter it, fully. You are not trying to solve their problem, but you are aiming to connect with another person. You are not playing therapist; you are having a guiding, supportive conversation. Focus on listening, pausing and giving space to the connection between you and the other person.

Skill 4 ('E'): Empower

1 Ask questions about their personal and external resources

2 Reaffirm their personal strengths

3 Support the person to identify their next steps

4 Collaboratively work on safety planning if needed

What have you tried so far ....?

How did that work for you .....?

Have you thought about talking to..........?

Have you spoken to ....your doctor, our

EAP, your partner, family, friends?

What support do you think would be best

for you right now............?

We could ....

What if I checked in with you............?

The final step in the S.A.F.E conversations framework is Empower.

The key theme here is that we are supporting the other person to empower themselves. We want to help the person identify their own resources and their own strengths and reach out for professional resources as required.

But what if the person does not want help? We will talk about this shortly.

In this fourth step we (gently) ask questions about their personal and external supports and resources. In other words, we are helping the person become aware of what is available, reaffirming their personal strengths, supporting them in identifying their next steps and then collaboratively working on safety planning and signposting additional resources, if required.

These are examples of questions that you could ask and adjust to your own style. The purpose of these questions is to support the person in creating awareness into their own situation.

- *What have you tried so far to help you through this?*
- *What have you done so far to solve this for yourself?*
- *How helpful was that for you?*
- *What resources have you used to support and help you?*
- *What has or hasn't worked in the past to support you during difficult times?*

If the person's awareness and use of resources is very low, then this is where it is very helpful to offer suggestions. But remember: we are not giving advice or telling them what to do.

There are three levels of support and resources that you can offer.

1. Level 1: Self and others
2. Level 2: Professional
3. Level 3: Crisis

I will explain each of these levels and types of support in more detail in Chapter 5, but here are some examples:

- Level 1: *Have you thought about taking a break and going for a quick walk, or reaching out to a friend or colleague that you feel comfortable speaking to about this situation?*
- Level 2: *Have you thought about talking to your doctor about what you're experiencing? Have you thought about talking to our Employee Assistance Provider?*
- Level 3 (please see Chapter 6 for more context on crisis situations)

Also, we could ask them some questions that might be more directional, like 'What support do you think would be best for you right now?'

If we do, it is very important to keep the focus on the 'you' to enable the person to be empowered to take their own actions. Be careful to avoid 'we' and 'I' questions (e.g. 'What can we do for you?' or 'What can I do for you?').

As a manager, it is important that you do not come in with the 'we' or the 'I' too early. Although it's nice to want to help someone, you've got to be aware that you may be disempowering the other person.

At some deep level, you are fundamentally saying, 'Look, you can't do this on your own – you need my help.' Also, it's putting the onus on the other person to come up with a solution rather than empowering them to find one and supporting them through that process.

REFLECT THEIR STRENGTHS

Be Authentic, Avoid Patronising

Challenges · Difficult · Enhance · Recognize · Being Aware · Develop · Assist · Focus · Responsibilities · Discover · Care · Attention · Identity · Caregiving · Experience · Caring · Reflection · Internal Resources · Take Control · Wellbeing · Ongoing Bemands · Competent · Capabilities · Action Plan

STRENGTHS

A wonderful gift that we give to another person when we care about them is to reflect their strengths. This is not done in a shallow patronising kind of way, like saying: *'You can get through this, _____, you'll get over it!'* (with a 'rah rah' and a pat on the back!).

Recognising and reaffirming the strengths in others is about noticing their traits, their character and their personality. You must see past all the exterior appearances and behaviours and 'see and feel' the 'essence' of the person. You must set an intention to do this with people and develop it over time.

Three key areas in which to develop this capability are:

1. Paying attention to how people approach challenges.
2. Observing how people communicate.
3. Recogising individual expertise.

HOW TO IDENTIFY AND ACKNOWLEDGE STRENGTHS IN OTHERS IN THE WORKPLACE

PAY ATTENTION TO HOW PEOPLE APPROACH CHALLENGES

Some people excel at problem-solving, while others thrive in fast-paced environments. When you observe someone overcoming obstacles, take note of the strategies they use and the skills they demonstrate. Recognize and celebrate their achievements, and encourage them to share their approach with others in the team.

OBSERVE HOW PEOPLE COMMUNICATE

Good communication is essential in any workplace. Look for individuals who are skilled at active listening, can express themselves clearly and succinctly, and can adapt their communication style to different audiences. These individuals are likely to be effective collaborators and valuable team members.

RECOGNIZE INDIVIDUAL EXPERTISE

Each person brings their unique strengths and knowledge to a team. Take the time to learn about each team member's background and expertise, and recognize their contributions to the team's success. Encourage them to share their knowledge with others and create opportunities for them to apply their skills in meaningful ways. By recognizing and valuing the individual strengths of team members, you can create a more engaged and motivated workforce.

As a non-work example, I once took a Lifeline caller who was a young guy who was really struggling. He said, 'Look, I am just going crazy. I have been driving around for hours. I want to see my girlfriend. She is sick in the hospital, but her mother will not let me see her.'

Let me ask you, the reader, the question: what are this guy's strengths?

When I use this example in my workshops, many people will respond with 'Not really sure' because they focus on his behaviour.

But here are examples of his strengths:

1. He has put up his hand to ask for help by ringing Lifeline.
2. He is very caring.
3. He is persistent.

I chose 'caring' and I reflected back to him, 'You sound like you are a really caring guy.'

When someone sees a strength in us and tells us something about ourselves that aligns to our identity of ourselves, it is a very powerful gift.

I also asked, 'How are you looking after yourself? How are you caring for you?'

Essentially what I was aiming to do was to help him come to his own self-awareness about his own self-care. He agreed and said, 'Yep, I need to go home, have a break, have some food, get some good sleep, and then wake up in a better state tomorrow.'

He also said, 'Thanks, Man, I hadn't really thought that about myself, but I guess I am a pretty caring sort of guy!' He now knows something about himself that he has probably never been told before.

When you empower another person in a genuine and authentic way, you give them a gift that touches their identity and their essence. We all have strengths and challenges. Sometimes our challenges are overused strengths.

I have had many Lifeline callers who are loving and caring people who feel used and betrayed because they give so much to other people who do not reciprocate their care and love. They are hurting because they hold such high expectations of others to love and care for them the way they do – and it does not happen.

One of the strategies that I consistently help them explore for themselves is setting personal boundaries. This is complicated and will often require a lot of discussion and self-awareness from a counsellor or clinical psychologist.

Follow Up and Support

People often ask 'Should I follow up?'. Definitely. When you follow up, you are not doing it from the perspective of 'stalking'. You do it because you care, and you want to support them on their improvement journey.

Overall, it's important to remember that mental health support is an ongoing process, and that employees may need different types of support at different times. By creating a supportive workplace culture and providing employees with resources and support, organisations and managers can help employees manage their mental health and thrive in the workplace – and beyond.

1. **Encourage open communication:** Create a S.A.F.E and supportive environment where employees feel comfortable talking about their mental health concerns. Encourage employees to come forward if they are struggling, and provide them with resources and support to manage their mental health.
2. **Provide access to mental health services:** Ensure that employees have access to mental health services, such as counseling or therapy, through an Employee Assistance Program or health insurance. Make sure that employees know how to access these resources and that they are confidential.

3. **Train managers and supervisors:** Provide training to managers and supervisors on how to recognise and respond to mental health concerns in their employees. This can include training on how to have conversations about mental health, how to accommodate employees who are struggling with mental health issues, and how to provide support and resources.

4. **Accommodate employee needs:** Work with employees who are struggling with mental health issues to provide adjustments that will help them manage their symptoms while still managing work. This may include flexible work arrangements, modified work duties or additional support or resources.

5. **Foster a supportive workplace culture:** Create a workplace culture that prioritises employee well-being and mental health. This can include promoting work-life balance, encouraging breaks and self-care, and reducing stigma around mental health.

What if the Person Keeps Coming to You for Help?

If you are starting to be concerned that someone is coming to you regularly for help, then it is important to ask them gently, 'Have you thought about talking to our Employee Assistance Provider, or your Doctor, to assist you?'

Let's imagine that they respond with something like, '*I feel safe talking with you; you know me, and I don't like to talk about this with strangers or a doctor.*'

Here you can try a gentle response like: 'I appreciate you have that trust in me, but I am not an expert in this area. If your symptoms are persisting, then it is recommended you see a healthcare professional, who can help you with these difficulties that you are experiencing'.

Please remember as always: the brain is just another body part! What would you be doing if the person was coming to you and talking about their back pain or their stomach pain?

What if the Person Does Not Want Help?

What are the reasons why someone would not want help?

> **Stigma:** What will people think of me?
> **Shame:** What is wrong with me? I am hopeless and a loser.
> **Confusion:** What is happening to me? Why am I feeling this way?
> **Reputation:** If I cannot handle the pressure, then I will lose my job.
> **Status:** What will people think of me if they find out that I have mental health issues and can't cope?
> **Rejection:** If I am struggling with my mental health, then I am weak, so I can't talk about it, or they might fire me or ostracise me.
> **Denial:** I am not the problem – other people are.
> **Bad Patch:** I'm just going through a bad patch at the moment – I will get over it.

The strategy when someone does not want help is not to push it. Otherwise, they get defensive and obstinate.

They will also likely have their personal stress reaction triggered. Therefore, they will either:

- **Fight:** externalise and blame others or circumstances. (It is my boss. It is the company. It is my work colleagues. It is the customers. It is my partner. It is my children. It is my parents.)
- **Flight:** internalise and shame themselves (I can't do this. I am hopeless. I am weak. I am letting everyone down. I will get sacked. I will never get promoted.)
- **Freeze:** avoid the conversation until their situation gets worse.

The strategy here is to ask gently what they are concerned about. If they open up and share with you, then you will hear their reasons.

Please be aware that these reasons may not 'make sense' or sound 'logical' to you, so do not be judgmental and condescending.

This is a person who is in mental and emotional pain. You would not say to someone who had a fractured ankle and was in pain: 'oh don't be silly – you'll get over it!

Stay compassionate and focused on helping them access their own support and resources that they are comfortable with.

If the person's behaviour is disruptive in the workplace or at home, you will be entering the complex territory of performance management in a work context, or relationship management in a family context.

These situations go beyond the scope of this book.

Some of these situations I cover in the half-day workshop, S.A.F.E Conversations at Work and in Life.

You would also learn how to handle crisis situations through Mental Health First Aid -Accreditation Training.

Or you can reach out to your Employee Assistance Program Coordinator or Doctor (see the next chapter).

A Summary of the Dos and Don'ts of S.A.F.E Conversations

DO'S

✓ Connect With Them. Let Them Know You Care And Are Concerned For Their Wellbeing

✓ Be Direct And Talk Honestly About Your Concerns (Asking Questions Shows That You Care)

✓ Listen, Non-judgmentally

✓ Allow Them To Express Their Feelings Without Challenge Or Debate

✓ Encourage Them To Seek Support And Get Help

✓ Ask What They Are Happy For You To Discuss With Others / Team. Respect Their Confidentiality

DON'T

✗ Do Not Show Any Feelings Of Surprise Or Shock

✗ If You Are Worried About Their Immediate Safety, Do Not Leave Them Alone

✗ Do Not Shoulder This Responsibility Yourself. Seek Advice, Support And Help

✗ Don't Diagnose, And Avoid Labels Ie. "Mental Illness"

✗ Don't Force Anyone To Get Help, You Can Only Discuss Options And Encourage It

CHAPTER 5

THE RESOURCES – TO ASSIST SOMEONE YOU CARE ABOUT, INCLUDING YOURSELF

"Self-care is never a selfish act - it is simply good stewardship of the only gift I have, the gift I was put on earth to offer to others."

– Parker Palmer

"Mental health is the key to a happy life, and it starts with loving yourself."

– Louise Hay

Comparing Physical First Aid and Mental First Aid

The table below shows a way of comparing physical first aid and mental health first aid.

Let's start with the example of a physical incident happening at work.

We would categorise the levels of severity and seriousness as:

Level 0.   no injuries
Level 1.   a cut requiring a bandage
Level 2.   an injury requiring medical attention
Level 3.   serious injury – calling 000

COMPARING PHYSICAL & MENTAL FIRST AID

Level	Physical First Aid	Mental Health First Aid	Strategies & Resources
0	No injuries	No signs or symptoms	16 Personal Self-Care Strategies for Zero Symptoms or Mild Symptoms • The Quick Eight (8) for Work • The Deep Eight (8) for Life
1	Cut that requires bandage	Mild signs & symptoms	16 Personal Self-Care Strategies for Zero Symptoms or Mild Symptoms • The Quick Eight (8) for Work • The Deep Eight (8) for Life
2	Injury requiring medical attention	Frequent signs & symptoms	Mental Health First Aider, Employee Assistance Provider, Doctor, Specialist
3	Serious injury - 000	Crisis signs & symptoms	Mental Health First Aider, EAP, Doctor, Specialist, 000

It's important to note that mental illness is a complex and multifaceted issue, and there is no single way to categorise or describe its severity. However, there are some commonly used categories to describe increasing levels of mental illness.

Level 0.   no signs and symptoms
Level 1.   mild signs and symptoms
Level 2.   significant signs and symptoms
Level 3.   severe/crisis signs and symptoms

The strategies and resources to support mental health first aid can be segmented into Levels 0 and 1 (the 16 personal self-care strategies) and Levels 2 and 3 (professional mental health resources).

Always remember: if symptoms persist, please see your healthcare professional.

16 Personal Self-Care Strategies

The 16 personal self-care strategies and resources that support Levels 0 and 1 of mental health illness/injury are applicable to any aspect of life in and out of the workplace. You can support yourself by applying them, and you can support your team members, colleagues, family and friends by encouraging them to incorporate these strategies and resources into their work and lives.

These 16 strategies can be divided into two categories: The Quick Eight (8) for Work and The Deep Eight (8) for Life.

THE QUICK 8 FOR WORK

Managing Mental Health While Working

BREAKS

TRIGGERS

BREATHE

MIND

FLUIDS

MOVE

SLEEP

RELATIONSHIPS

These 'Quick Eight' personal strategies stem from evidence-based best practice and can help you and others maintain good mental health at work.

1. Breaks: Take a break, manage your energy and check in with your mood. If you start to feel depleted, then reenergise with a break.

2. Triggers: Notice what and who triggers you, and take stock of your personal stress reactions. Understanding the root causes of your stress/distress helps you be better prepared to manage it, and seek help if it persists.

Examples of triggers could be:

    a. Not setting priorities and experiencing overwhelm. Prioritising your tasks can help you manage your time more effectively and reduce the feeling of being overwhelmed.

    b. Not setting boundaries. Setting boundaries with your managers, colleagues and family can help you maintain a healthy work-life balance and reduce stress.

3. Breathing: Down-regulate your personal stress reaction through the breath. Do conscious, intentional big belly breaths when in meetings and when on Zoom/Teams calls, or any work situation that causes you stress.

4. Thought patterns: Notice your positive and negative thoughts and feelings. Positive thinking can improve your stress reaction coping skills. If you're finding it difficult to distance yourself from the negative thoughts, try reframing/reappraising a situation from a different perspective and focus only on finding positive aspects about it. By developing and practising a positive mindset, we improve our ability to adapt and bounce forward from stress, adversity and difficult work situations.

5. Fluids: Keep your body and brain hydrated with water and unsweetened tea. Coffee can work, too, but too much caffeine isn't helpful for other reasons (like disturbing your sleeping habits). Limit the sugary juices and sodas, as well.

6. Move: Take a walk or stand up in meetings. If you work from home or have flexible hours, schedule time for a workout or some stretching to break up your time and have a moment of screen detox.

7. Sleep: Getting enough sleep is essential for physical and mental well-being, and will help you perform better at work.

8. Positive Relationships: Maintain good relationships through gratitude and appreciation. Disengage from toxic work dynamics. Building and maintaining positive relationships with colleagues can help reduce stress and improve mental health. Don't be afraid to seek support from colleagues, managers or mental health professionals when you need it. And if someone comes to you, be curious and empathetic, not judgmental!

THE DEEP 8 FOR LIFE

Eight Personal Strategies to Self-Care/Self-Nourish/Self-loveto Maintain Good Mental and Emotional Health & Support Others

EAT WELL	**MOVE & EXERCISE**	**MAINTAIN POSITIVE RELATIONSHIPS**	**SLEEP 7+ HOURS**
DO 3 GRATITUDES PER DAY	**DEVELOP A MINDFULNESS-MEDITATION PRACTICE**	**FINDING MEANING AND PURPOSE**	**MANAGE YOUR ADDICTIONS**

These 'Deep Eight' strategies can help you practise self-care, self-nourishment, and self-love to enhance your well-wellbeing and happiness in and beyond the workplace.

1. Eating well: Eating balanced, health-promoting and nutritious food can help improve physical and mental health, and boost energy levels. What we put into our mouths eventually goes up into our brains. Our gut and brain are directly connected, so what happens in your stomach affects what happens in your brain. Notice what impact the foods you eat and the fluids you drink are having on your brain's (and your body's) performance, energy levels and moods.

2. Physical activity and exercise: The recommended amount of exercise for good mental health varies depending on lots of individual factors like age, overall health, mobility and fitness levels. However, general guidelines suggest that the average adult should aim for at least 150 minutes of moderate aerobic exercise or 75 minutes of vigorous aerobic exercise per week along with muscle-strengthening activities at least two days per week.

Moderate-intensity aerobic exercise includes activities such as brisk walking, cycling or swimming, which increase heart rate and breathing, but still allow for conversation.

Vigorous-intensity aerobic exercise includes activities such as running, cycling uphill or playing sports, which increase heart rate and breathing to the point where speaking full sentences is difficult.

It is also recommended that individuals incorporate a variety of exercise types into their routine, including cardiovascular exercise, strength training, and flexibility and balance exercises.

While the recommended amount of exercise may seem daunting, it is important to note that even small amounts of physical activity can have mental health benefits. Research has shown that just 10–15 minutes of moderate-intensity exercise can improve mood and reduce symptoms of anxiety and depression.

WHY DOES EXERCISE IMPROVE MENTAL HEALTH?

BOOSTING
Boosting neurotransmitters: Exercise has been shown to increase the production of neurotransmitters such as endorphins, dopamine, and serotonin, which are associated with feelings of happiness and well-being.

REDUCING
Reducing inflammation: Exercise can also help reduce inflammation in the body, which has been linked to depression and other mental health conditions.

IMPROVING
Improving brain function: Regular physical activity has been shown to improve brain function, including increased blood flow to the brain and improved cognitive function.

REDUCING
Reducing stress: Exercise can also help reduce stress and anxiety by releasing tension in the muscles and promoting relaxation.

PROVIDING
Providing a sense of accomplishment: Exercise can provide a sense of accomplishment and self-confidence, which can contribute to improved mental health and well-being.

3. Positive relationships: Positive relationships are essential to good mental health for several reasons. Humans are social creatures, and our connections with others are fundamental to our well-being. Positive relationships provide emotional support, companionship and a sense of belonging, which are all important for our mental health.

Research has shown that positive relationships can lead to a range of benefits, including increased happiness, reduced stress and better physical health. On the other hand, social isolation and loneliness have been linked to several negative mental health outcomes, including depression, anxiety and cognitive decline, including dementia.

One of the key researchers in this area is John Bowlby. Bowlby was a British psychologist and psychiatrist who is best known for his work on attachment theory. He argued that humans have an innate need for attachment and that our early relationships with caregivers have a profound impact on our mental health and well-being.

Barbara Fredrickson is a positive psychology researcher who proposed the 'broaden-and-build' theory of positive emotions. Her work on positivity ratios suggests that a ratio of at least three positive emotions to every negative emotion (3-to-1) is necessary for individuals to flourish and experience good mental health. This positivity ratio has been linked to increased resilience, improved cognitive functioning and better physical health.

The work of both of these researchers highlights the importance of cultivating positive emotions in daily life to improve overall well-being.

4. Sleep is very important: There is now a substantial body of research that recommends most adults need 7–9 hours of sleep per night.

If you are getting less than that, then it would be wise to notice what's happening in your brain and body when you are not getting enough sleep. Notice your exhaustion. Notice how you might crave more coffee, sugar and food that may not be good for you. Notice if your personal stress reaction activates and you are more angry, anxious or avoidant. Notice how you might be nodding off and having micro-sleeps (not a good way to operate in a fast-moving world!).

Sleep is like gym for the brain. The brain needs sleep for several reasons, and research has shown that sleep is crucial for maintaining healthy brain function. During sleep, the brain is actively engaged in a range of restorative processes that are necessary for optimal cognitive and emotional functioning.

WHY DO OUR BRAINS NEED SLEEP?

MEMORY CONSOLIDATION

Sleep plays a critical role in consolidating memories and information learned during waking hours. During sleep, the brain processes and consolidates memories, allowing them to be stored and retrieved more easily.

NEURAL REPAIR

Sleep also promotes the repair and restoration of brain cells and tissues. During sleep, the brain produces proteins that help repair and regenerate cells, which is important for maintaining healthy brain function.

WHY DO OUR BRAINS NEED SLEEP?

EMOTIONAL REGULATION

Sleep is also essential for regulating emotions and processing emotional experiences. Research has shown that sleep helps reduce emotional reactivity and improves emotional regulation, which is important for overall mental health.

CLEARING WASTE PRODUCTS

During sleep, the brain also flushes out waste products that accumulate during waking hours. This waste clearance process is crucial for maintaining healthy brain function and has been linked to a range of cognitive and neurological disorders.

What if poor sleep is impacting your mental health?

There are several things you can do to improve your sleep hygiene and promote better sleep:

- **Stick to a consistent sleep schedule.** Try to go to bed and wake up at the same time each day, even on weekends. This helps regulate your body's internal clock and can improve the quality of your sleep.
- **Create a relaxing bedtime routine.** Establish a relaxing routine before bed that can help you wind down and prepare for sleep. This could include activities such as taking a warm bath, reading a book or practicing relaxation techniques like deep breathing or meditation.
- **Make sure your sleep environment is conducive to sleep.** Ensure that your bedroom is cool, quiet, dark and free from distractions like electronics or pets.
- **Limit caffeine and alcohol intake.** Avoid consuming caffeine or alcohol in the hours leading up to bedtime, as they can interfere with sleep.
- **Exercise regularly.** Regular exercise can help promote better sleep, but try to avoid exercising within a few hours of bedtime.
- **Seek professional help.** If poor sleep continues to impact your mental health, it may be helpful to seek professional help from a healthcare provider or mental health professional.

5. Gratitude: Do three Gs a day – three gratitudes per day. If you want to transition and change your life, start a gratitude practice and journaling. I tested this practice many years ago. I was in a sad and grumpy phase in my life, and so I started doing gratitude work. I would do it in bed before going to sleep. I would have a small book and I would write down three things that I was grateful for that day. I did that consistently over about three weeks, and I started to notice my mood change for the better. I have been doing this as a consistent practice now for many years – something that I do every day. I do not necessarily write all the time, but I am constantly in a state of gratitude and appreciation for life.

Why does it work and what is the science behind it?

There is a substantial body of research these days that highlights the importance of gratitude (and a great attitude!).

Our brains are a meaning-making and prediction-making machine, and what we focus on will grow in our awareness. From the moment we are born and in utero, our brains are taking in sights, sounds and feelings in the body and making meaning of them. As we get older and function as children, adolescents and then adults, this process continues. What we place our awareness on will expand and grow in our minds.

If you place your awareness on all the negativity that exists in the world, and you keep looking at the negative news and toxic social media, then your view of the world will reflect that ('Yep the world is f..#@ and people are bad.'). This perspective is very toxic, and it is not good for your mental and emotional health.

However, if you start to notice the good things in life; if you are grateful; if you are appreciative; if you start saying 'thank you' to your partner and to your children and to your work colleagues; if you see the beauty in nature and in life...then you will fill your brain with positivity and hope and gratitude.

Yes, the tough stuff does still exist – accidents happen, wars happen, people practise bad behaviour. However, when you fortify your brain with positivity practices, then you have a stronger brain to deal with and solve the challenging and complex problems we have.

6. Mindfulness and meditation: Similar to the substantial amount of research into sleep and positive relationships, practising mindfulness meditation practice is not 'woo-woo' stuff. These practices have been shown to be important for mental and emotional health in several ways:

1. To reduce stress and anxiety by promoting relaxation and increasing feelings of calmness.
2. To improve our ability to regulate emotions by allowing us to observe our thoughts and feelings without judgment, which in turn helps us respond more effectively to challenging situations.
3. To enhance our attention and focus, which leads to improvements in cognitive functioning and productivity.
4. To increase compassion and empathy, which can improve social relationships and overall well-being.

When you learn to soothe, connect, look after yourself and care about others, then this is not 'woo-woo'. It is using our brilliant brains in an effective and powerful way for a happy life and making a positive contribution to humanity and the planet.

If you're interested in learning more about this practise, I encourage you to watch this short video, Neuroscience of Mindfulness Meditation in Four Minutes:
https://www.youtube.com/watch?v=vo_VANW35b0.

Here are two examples of mindfulness and meditation practices that are easy and practical. I invite you to try them on, for a few minutes. Don't expect magic immediately! Make a commitment to a couple of weeks, and don't worry about your racing brain – it will settle down over time.

1. **Mindful breathing:** This is a simple but effective mindfulness practice that involves focusing on your breath. Find a quiet place to sit or lie down and close your eyes (closing the eyes is just useful to cut out looking at things, which will distract you). Begin to breathe slowly

and deeply while focusing on the sensation of the breath moving in and out of your body. If your mind starts to wander, gently bring your attention back to your breath. You can do this practice for a few minutes, or as long as you like.

2. Body scan meditation: This is a mindfulness practice that involves paying attention to different parts of your body. Find a comfortable place to sit or lie down and close your eyes. Begin to focus on your breath, then bring your attention to your toes. Notice any sensations in your toes, then move your attention up to your feet, ankles and so on, scanning your body from head to toe. If you notice any tension or discomfort in any part of your body, simply observe it without judgment. You can do this practice for a few minutes, or as long as you like.

7. Finding meaning and purpose. Engaging in work or activities that provide a sense of purpose and meaning can improve mental and emotional well-being. Accessing what we enjoy though hobbies, creativity and self-expression will often provide us with a sense of happiness and fulfilment.

There are many different ways that we can find meaning and purpose in our lives. I call them 'love sources' – ways in which we can self-nourish and bring authentic self-love into our lives. Some examples are:

- Set meaningful goals. Identify what is important to you and set goals that align with those values. This can give you a sense of direction and purpose.
- Cultivate positive relationships. Nurture healthy relationships with family, friends and colleagues. Strong connections with others can bring a sense of belonging and purpose to your life.
- Find a meaningful career. Pursue work that aligns with your passions and values. When you feel fulfilled in your work, it can bring a sense of purpose and satisfaction.
- Volunteer and give back. Helping others can be a

meaningful way to contribute to society and make a positive impact in the world.

- Engage in activities that bring you joy. Whether it's a hobby, sport, or creative pursuit, finding something you enjoy and spending time doing it can bring a sense of fulfillment and purpose.
- Practise gratitude. Focusing on what you are grateful for can help you appreciate the good things in your life and bring a sense of purpose, as well as strengthening you through the difficult times which will surely happen.
- Reflect on your values. Take time to think about what is important to you and how you can align your actions with those values. This can give you a sense of direction and purpose in life.

8. Manage your addictions. We all have addictions, and they all vary in intensity and impact. Many times, our use of substances and behaviours are coping strategies to deal with our mental and emotional pain – whether we are conscious or unconscious of what we are doing. Hence, an important starting point to managing your addictions – and caring for yourself through them – is self-compassion and awareness of your own sense of self-identity. If the duration, impact or severity of your addictions persists or increases, please see your healthcare professional.

The Role of Mental Health First Aiders

Mental Health First Aid (MHFA) is an internationally recognised training program that aims to increase mental health literacy and build mental health resilience in the community. In recent years, there has been growing interest in the role of MHFA in the workplace, and research has explored the potential benefits of having MHFAers in the workplace.

Studies suggest that having MHFAers in the workplace can improve mental health awareness, reduce stigma surrounding mental health and increase access to support and resources for employees who may be experiencing mental health challenges. MHFAers can also play a critical role in identifying and responding to early warning signs of mental health issues, providing initial support and guiding employees to appropriate resources for help.

Research has also shown that MHFAers can help to create a culture of mental health safety in the workplace, where employees feel comfortable talking about mental health and seeking support when needed. This can lead to improved productivity, reduced absenteeism and overall better mental health outcomes for employees.

However, it is important to note that MHFAers are not a substitute for professional mental health care, and their role is primarily focused on providing initial support and guiding employees to appropriate resources. It is also important to ensure that MHFAers receive ongoing training and support to ensure that they are equipped to fulfill their role effectively.

Professional Mental Health Resources

If you or someone you know is experiencing significant or severe symptoms of mental illness/injury (Levels 2 and 3), professional mental health resources are the best support.

As always, our mantra is: *'If symptoms persist, please see your Health care Professional'*. If a person's situation is indicative of signs and symptoms that are impacting on their work, relationships and life, then we would encourage them to consider accessing professional resources.

It is not our place to be diagnosing, but encouraging.

Each individual will make their own decision regarding this type of support, if they seek it out and what it looks like if they do; we can't make them do it.

There are four main sources of professional help we can refer them to:

1. Workplace Employee Assistance Provider [EAP].
2. Healthcare providers (doctors, primary care providers, psychologists, counsellors, psychiatrists, clinical social workers and peer support specialists).
3. Helplines.
4. Online resources.

PROFESSIONAL RESOURCES FOR LEVELS 2 AND 3

Beyond Blue

Australian Human Rights Commission

World Health Organization

Black Dog Institute

REACH OUT.COM

healthdirect Australia

WayAhead
Mental Health Association NSW

Heads ûp

mind
for better mental health

Mental Health Australia

Mental Health Foundation of New Zealand

Mental Health Foundation Australia

Lifeline Saving Lives
Crisis Support. Suicide Prevention.

The EAP: Employee Assistance Program/Provider

Many companies offer the services of an Employee Assistance Program/Provider.

It will be very helpful, particularly if you are a manager, that you familiarise yourself with this service, so that you know what the experience is like and how it works.

Imagine that you might be having a S.A.F.E conversation (the second or third check in) with a team member who has been struggling or troubled with a mental/emotional difficulty.

During the conversation, you identify that they have tried some of the 'Quick Eight' or 'Deep Eight' strategies, but their challenges are continuing or persisting.

Then you might ask, 'Have you thought about reaching out to our Employee Assistance Provider, who has a range of specialists in these areas?'

If they then asked you *'What's it like, and how can they help me?'*

And your response is something like 'I don't know, but I have heard it is very good'.

Then your credibility goes through the floor!

Therefore, if you are a manager, it can be very helpful if you use the Employee Assistance Program service yourself, so you know what it is.

Some people may be reluctant based on the perceived issues of privacy and confidentiality. But Employee Assistance Program providers do not give names to the companies that they work for.

Medical Professionals

If they wish to talk to their own doctor or primary care provider, then encourage the person to make an appointment with a person who specialises in adult mental health so they are well-equipped to understand the situation and more likely to have a network of professionals for more specialised referrals.

The primary care provider will be the access point to all other medical professional specialists, such as clinical psychologists, counsellors, psychiatrists, clinical social workers and peer support specialists.

Helplines

What happens if you can't get an appointment for weeks, you can't afford one or you need immediate assistance?

Medical resources everywhere are under substantial pressure, and the same is true with mental/emotional health resources and support.

For all short-term and acute needs, we recommend that you use free resources like Lifeline, Beyond Blue, 1800 Respect, Black Dog, Mensline and Kidsline. In the event of an emergency, or if you are concerned for the safety of yourself of someone else, you should always call 000 or your local emergency services number.

I cover more about this in Chapter 7.

If you have more specialised needs, these main helplines can also refer you to hotlines and specialists with expertise in specific communities and support needs (e.g. LGBTQIA+, BIPOC/BAME, veterans, living alone, post-partum depression etc.).

Many months ago, a friend of mine was going through a very difficult time following the break-up of a relationship. He was having severe suicidal thoughts, and besides talking with me and his psychologist, I encouraged him to call Lifeline regularly – which he did three times a day for a few days to get support to help him through his acute emotional pain.

Healing and recovery from mental and emotional wounds takes as long or longer than physical wounds and illnesses, and so it is important to use a whole range of professional, social and personal resources.

SUPPORT RESOURCES

If you or anyone you know needs help

LIFELINE 13 11 14

KIDS HELPLINE 1800 551 800

MENSLINE AUSTRALIA 1300 789 978

SUICIDE CALL BACK SERVICE 1300 659 467

BEYOND BLUE 1300 224 636

HEADSPACE 1800 650 890

ReachOut at **AU.REACHOUT.COM**

CARE LEAVERS AUSTRALASIA NETWORK (CLAN) 1800 008 774

Online Resources

The top five online resources in Australia for mental health support that have been recommended by mental health professionals and organisations are:

1. **Lifeline:** Lifeline is a national charity providing 24/7 crisis support and suicide prevention services in Australia. They offer a range of online and telephone support services, including a crisis chat service and telephone counseling.
2. **Beyond Blue:** Beyond Blue is a national mental health organisation that provides information, resources and support for individuals experiencing mental health challenges. They offer a range of online resources, including forums, web chat and phone support.
3. **Headspace:** Headspace is an Australian youth mental health foundation that provides early intervention mental health services to people ages 12–25. They offer a range of online resources, including information on mental health, tools and resources for young people and their families.
4. **Black Dog Institute:** The Black Dog Institute is a research organisation that focuses on mental health research, education and treatment. They offer a range of online resources, including self-help tools, courses and webinars.
5. **SANE Australia:** SANE Australia is a national mental health charity that provides support, information and resources to people affected by complex mental health issues. They offer a range of online resources, including fact sheets, online forums and a helpline.

Lived Experience Specialists

Lived experience specialists are individuals and organisations who have personal experience with mental health challenges and recovery, and who use their knowledge and expertise to support others who are also going through similar experiences. They can assist people in recovery with mental health difficulties in several ways, including:

1. **Providing hope and inspiration:** Lived experience specialists can offer a positive role model for those in recovery, as they can demonstrate that it is possible to live a fulfilling life despite experiencing mental health challenges.
2. **Peer support:** Lived experience specialists can provide peer support to individuals in recovery. They can listen to and empathize with the struggles of others, and offer insights based on their own experiences.
3. **Sharing coping strategies:** Lived experience specialists can offer practical advice and coping strategies based on their own experiences, which may be helpful for individuals who are struggling with similar issues.
4. **Advocacy:** Lived experience specialists can advocate for the needs of individuals with mental health difficulties, and help to reduce the stigma and discrimination that can be associated with mental health challenges.
5. **Education and awareness:** Lived experience specialists can help to raise awareness about mental health issues and the importance of seeking treatment, as well as educate others about the recovery process.

Overall, lived experience specialists can play an important role in supporting individuals in recovery with mental health difficulties, and can help to promote hope, healing, and resilience.

Examples of such organisations are : The Women's Resilience Centre, Roses in the Ocean, SANE Australia, BeyondBlue, Headspace and Black Dog Institute.

CHAPTER 6

CRISIS SUPPORT – WHAT IF THE PERSON IS IN CRISIS?

"The greatest glory in living lies not in never falling, but in rising every time we fall."

— Nelson Mandela

Author's note:

The information provided here is for educational purposes only and is not intended as a substitute for professional clinical diagnosis or treatment. This material is not intended to be used for self-diagnosis or to replace the advice of a qualified healthcare professional. If you are experiencing mental health concerns, please seek the guidance of a licensed mental health provider.

If this material triggers some uncomfortable emotions for you, then we encourage you please to seek appropriate support. This support could be with a family member, friend, colleague or a helpline such as Beyond Blue (on 1300 22 4636), Lifeline (on 13 11 14), your Employee Assistance Provider or your doctor.

What do you do if the person you want to talk to, or are talking to – is at Level 3 of mental health illness/injury and is showing signs of being in crisis, such as having suicidal thoughts, engaging in self-harm (non-suicidal self-injury), having severe panic attacks or experiencing psychosis?

This level of support is definitely the one where you absolutely need professional training to manage (such as Mental Health First Aid Accreditation Training or a crisis-informed program like ASIST – Applied Suicide Intervention Skills Training).

There are complicated reasons as to why a person would get to a place of crisis, and one perspective is through the lens of DIS: Duration, Impact and Severity (Chapter 2).

As an example, I recently had a Lifeline caller who was upset because he was having frequent arguments and fights with his partner.

He called because he felt so low and was having suicidal thoughts.

When I spent some time talking with him, he shared how he was grieving the death of his father, who had died overseas during COVID-19, and he did not get to be with him before his death. This was very sad.

But as I continued talking with him, the deeper grief that needed healing in this man was that his father was an angry man with high expectations, and he never felt that his father loved him. He never felt that he lived up to his father's expectations.

When we experience deep grief and sadness from emotional loss – which has duration and severity– then this will be very mentally and emotionally injurious.

The people who are at highest risk are those who have an internalising personal stress/threat reaction. As we have seen, these people internalise their thoughts and feelings and feel they are not good enough, not worthy enough or not loved.

When they have increasing acute stress, like fractured relationships, all of these injuries can compound each other, and their thoughts and feelings can become suicidal.

It is critically important that if you think that someone may be suicidal that you ask them directly if they are having suicidal thoughts.

What I am about to share with you is a guideline – based on hundreds of hours of best-practice training and experience. If you yourself or someone you know is having suicidal thoughts, our strong recommendation is that you get the assistance of Lifeline 131114, your EAP, or emergency service.

There are three reasons why people are often afraid of asking 'the suicide question':

1. They think that by asking the question it will put the idea into the person's head. Here is the fact: research has identified that if a person is not thinking of suicide, they will not think, 'Ah, not a bad idea – I hadn't been thinking about that, and now I am!'
2. People are concerned that if they ask the question, the person will get angry at them. This can happen because sometimes people ask the question in a very blaming or shaming kind of way like, 'You're not having any stupid thoughts like killing yourself, are you?'. That is a very hurtful and insensitive way to broach the topic.
3. People are concerned about if they get a 'yes' response and what they should do from there.

Here is a way to ask the question well that is based on best practice.

How to Ask Someone if They Are Having Suicidal Thoughts

Firstly, give the question context and reflect back the person's situation. Then ask the question directly.

When a person goes through the real emotional pain of a relationship break-up and issues of access to the kids, it can be so painful for them that they can often have thoughts of suicide. Have you been having thoughts of suicide?

This is a very gentle way of asking. It validates to the person that they are going through a really difficult situation. It normalises to them that they are not 'crazy', 'stupid' or 'weak' because other people in similar situations can experience very difficult thoughts and feelings, like wanting to escape from the emotional pain.

BEYOND BLUE - EMOTIONAL PAIN CAN BE A SIGNIFICANT FACTOR IN SUICIDAL THOUGHTS AND BEHAVIOURS

> Beyond Blue is an Australian mental health organization that conducts research and provides support to individuals and families affected by mental health conditions. Beyond Blue has conducted research into suicide and emotional pain and has identified a range of factors that can contribute to suicide risk.

> According to Beyond Blue, emotional pain can be a significant factor in suicidal thoughts and behaviours. Emotional pain can include feelings of hopelessness, helplessness, worthlessness, loneliness, and isolation. Individuals experiencing emotional pain may also have difficulty regulating their emotions and may experience intense feelings of sadness, anger, or anxiety.

> Beyond Blue's research has also identified a range of risk factors for suicide, including mental health conditions such as depression and anxiety, substance abuse, chronic pain, relationship breakdowns, financial difficulties, and a history of trauma or abuse. Additionally, social factors such as unemployment, social isolation, and discrimination can also contribute to suicide risk.

Beyond Blue's research identified that people do not fundamentally want to die: they want to be free of their emotional pain.

So, if they say 'yes' to having suicidal thoughts:

- Stay calm. They have the deep suffering, not you.
- Validate their feelings. (That must be very painful for you to be having those thoughts and feelings.)
- Ask gently about:
  - The frequency of the thoughts. (How often have you been having the thoughts of suicide? When was the last time you had the thoughts?)
  - Plans. (Have you made any plans? Have you established a means to do it? Where is that means now?)
- Offer support. (I would like to support you and help you. Who in your family or friends can you reach out to, so they can be with you now and go with you to your doctor or to the hospital?)

If you encounter any resistance, you could ask:

Would you be okay if we reached out to Lifeline, Beyond Blue or our EAP for assistance, because I would really like to support you and help you?

As you can see, this conversation is not an easy thing to do. Ideally, you need to be trained properly in mental health first aid. There you will have the opportunity to practise these conversations and crisis support in a learning context so that you develop your skills to down-regulate your stress reaction and keep a level head in order to help and support the person. You would also learn how to handle other crisis situations, such as where a person is self-harming, having panic attacks or experiencing psychosis.

I have the point of view that every manager on the planet, every parent, every teacher and every lecturer should be trained to notice the signs and symptoms, ask 'the suicide question', and know how to help.

Seven (7) men and two (2) women per day in Australia die by suicide. This training could go a long way in saving more lives.

CHAPTER 7

SUMMARY AND OPTIONS

"Happiness is not something ready-made. It comes from your own actions."

— Dalai Lama XIV

"The only way to do great work is to love what you do."

— Steve Jobs

I have a big HOPE [Holding On to Positive Expectations], that **S.A.F.E Conversations for Work and Life** makes a contribution as an early intervention strategy and skill set to help more people become aware of and access the support and resources they need to live the happy and authentic lives they are born to live.

This visual summary of S.A.F.E conversations shows the steps, the process and the examples of questions for each step.

If you scan the QR code on the back cover of the book, you will also be able to access more supporting resources.

S.A.F.E CONVERSATIONS FOR WORK AND LIFE™
EXAMPLE QUESTIONS

S. SELF AND OTHER AWARENESS

PHASE

Key Skills – Positive intention, genuine care

PROCESS

- Awareness of yourself and others
- Connect to build trust and rapport
- Be genuine and non-judgemental
- Choose appropriate time and place

EXAMPLES

Prepare for the conversation – are you in the right frame of mind?
Do you have the time?
Consider the other person and their situation
Where will you have the conversation?
How will you open the conversation and make a genuine connection?
Hi, how is...............?
Would you like to........?
Do you have time for a............?

A. ACKNOWLEDGE & ASK

PHASE

Key Skills – Open & closed questions, empower listening, perspective listening

PROCESS

- Inquire respectfully into the person's situation
- Use listening skills to build empathy
- Be aware of stigma, bias and judgement
- Be compassionate and allow the person to talk - if they want to

EXAMPLES

How is...............?
What have you been...................?
What's happening?
I wanted to let you know.................?
Are you ok? I'd just noticed..........?
Are you able to access the resources that could help you....?

F. FOCUS ON LISTENING

PHASE

Key Skills – Reflection of feelings, acknowledging, normalising, open & closed questions, empower listening

PROCESS

- Reflect what you are hearing - using their words
- Acknowledge the challenges the person is experiencing
- Be present with the person, and don't try to solve their problem or give advice

EXAMPLES

That must be............
I can see that would be........
You seem............
It sounds like you're feeling ...
Would you like to talk about that ....?

E. EMPOWER

PHASE

Key Skills – Strengths building, normalising, acknowledging, paraphrasing, open & closed questions, summarising & closing, knowledge of resources

PROCESS

- Identify personal and external resources
- Reaffirm their personal strengths
- Support the person to identify their next steps
- Collaboratively work on safety planning if needed

EXAMPLES

What have you tried before ....?
Do you think that...........?
Have you thought about talking to..........?
What support do you think will help you .....?
We could..............
What if I checked in with you............?
Thanks for..........., let's catch up again to...

I facilitate a wide range of workshops in this field as well as in other professional development areas – both in-person workshops and virtual interactive workshops.

The QR code on the back cover and the list of available programs below will give you more information if you would like to explore your mental health training and first aid needs further.

Option One: The Workshop

(S.A.F.E Conversation Skills for Managers and Teams). The mental health and wellbeing conversation skills for managers.

A three (3) hour workshop, in person or virtually via Zoom or Teams

- **Quick summary:** This workshop teaches managers and team members how to provide appropriate assistance to others who might be struggling with mental/emotional challenges or unwellness, or who sustain a mental/emotional injury (e.g. death of a loved one, a breakup, workplace stressors and harassment, etc.)
- **Longer summary:** Most managers and people do not have the skills to deal with these complex personal situations. In this workshop, attendees are taught to notice the signs that a person may be struggling and how to engage in a compassionate, person-centered conversation to empower the person to seek the assistance, support or resources they need. It does not teach them to be therapists or problem-solvers, and it helps them break down fears around saying 'the wrong thing'. It also helps people separate out the performance issues from the personal issues, be authentically caring and contribute significantly to creating a more engaged and committed workplace and community culture.

- **Key learning objectives:**

  1. How to identify the signs of mental and emotional unwellness
  2. How to approach a team member (what to say and what not to say)
  3. How to have a caring conversation
  4. How to help the person come to their own awareness
  5. How to know what resources to refer to
  6. How to manage your own self-care and the rest of the team

- **Feedback from past participants:**

  - *Bill is a very engaging authentic presenter, bringing to life an understanding of complex conditions with clear steps for action. I feel confident in what to do, how to approach and the importance of self-care.*
  - *This was an excellent course, which gave me more understanding of mental health and the confidence to address issues with our people and team.*
  - *Bill's facilitation, passion and stories were incredibly engaging and highly effective in helping us understand, along with delicate delivery of some very tough content.*
  - *Informative, amazing, humbling. Great facilitator, genuine, leaving me wanting to know more.*
  - *Interesting, informative and useful, with practical tools to apply in work and non-work scenarios. Thanks, Bill, for presenting this info with such care and respect.*
  - *I thought it was excellent, relevant and very well presented, thank you, Bill. We have a simple methodology to follow, and we have a clear way to empower our teams.*
  - *This was very positive, engaging and motivating, and Bill helped us feel like we can make a difference.*

Option Two: Train the Trainer
for S.A.F.E Conversation Skills Two-day program

If you have a larger organisation or government department, we have the option for you of training your key champions over a two-day 'train the trainer' program. This will teach your champions to deliver the program in-house for your company/division/department.

For details of this program, please contact
Bill Carson on +61 425 555 268

Option Three: The Online Course
One-hour online course

You can access this short online version of the course via the QR code on the back cover of this book.

Option Four: The Combination for Managers and Team Members
(S.A.F.E Conversation Skills for Managers, and Mental Health Awareness & Resources for Team Members)

The purpose of this option is that it gives HR, P&C or WHS Managers the option to have a combination of mental health conversation skills training for managers and general employee mental health awareness building.

The S.A.F.E conversations course is delivered as specified in Option 1.

The Mental Health Awareness & Resources for Teams can also be delivered in person or virtually (or as a hybrid). This 1.5-hour workshop provides a foundation and framework for assisting team members in understanding and caring for their mental and emotional well-being in the context of working in an office, at a worksite, at home or in a hybrid format.

Team members will learn practical tools and techniques to engage successfully in their work environments while recognising the potential challenges as well. Acknowledging that communication is critical in maintaining connections, especially during challenging times, team members will be given the tools to recognise their own signs of struggling, coping and thriving as well as a range of resources for their own self-care and mental well-being.

Key learning objectives:

1. How to recognise common responses to change, uncertainty, stress and isolation
2. How to identify signs when we might be struggling with work in the virtual world or the in-office/onsite world
3. How to adopt techniques and communication best-practice to enable productive working while maintaining well-being
4. How to explore and utilise a range of support options
5. How to apply strategies to care for yourself successfully

Feedback from past participants: 93% of 55 respondents said that they would be highly likely to recommend this program.

- *Training was great and very worthwhile. Bill was very engaging and made it interesting.*
- *Bill was accepting of thoughts and feelings. No judgement. Easy to listen to. Course flowed and stayed engaging.*
- *I learnt to make better choices/decisions, changing negative to positive, that are within my own control.*
- *Take time to eat healthier and make sure I do some exercise to maintain my own health. Try not to work past normal work times.*

Option Five: Mental Health First Aid - Accreditation Training

Several delivery options (Blended delivery could be a one day workshop plus 5–7 hours of blended e-learning OR Two 2.5–3 hour interaction workshops plus the e-learning; OR In-person delivery over a two-day workshop)

- Quick summary: This certification course teaches you how to provide initial support to other adults who may be experiencing a mental health problem or mental health crisis until appropriate professional help is received, or the crisis resolves, using a practical, evidence-based action plan.

- Longer summary: Around 1 in 5 Australian adults experience a diagnosable mental illness each year. Mental Health First Aid (MHFA) training teaches you practical skills to support someone experiencing mental health challenges. This skill set enables you to make a real difference at work and in your personal life. This course is based on guidelines developed through the expert consensus of mental health professionals and people with lived experience of mental health challenges and professional help. The mental health challenges covered include depression, anxiety, psychosis, substance use problems, eating disorders and gambling problems. The mental health crises covered include suicidal thoughts and behaviours, non-suicidal self-injury, panic attacks, traumatic events, severe psychotic states, aggressive behaviours and severe effects from alcohol or other drug use. This course is not therapy or a support group; it will help people separate out the performance issues from the personal issues, be authentically caring and contribute significantly to creating a more engaged and committed culture.

- **Key learning objectives:**

  1. Improve knowledge of mental illnesses, treatments and first aid actions
  2. Increase confidence in providing mental first aid
  3. Decrease stigmatising attitudes
  4. Increase the support provided to others

- **What you get:**

  1. You become an Accredited Mental Health First Aider after completing an online assessment.
  2. You receive an up-to-date manual of evidence-based practices.
  3. You receive additional resources to assist you in implementing and integrating Mental Health First Aid into your workplace.

- **Feedback from past participants:**

  - *Excellent – a course that as many people as possible should be doing. Should be mandatory in all workplaces to have mental health first aid officers.*
  - *Bill was an excellent facilitator and coach, taking the time to ensure everyone was clear and on the journey. He allowed space for questions and time to think, which are key when learning effectively online.*
  - *Bill was very good – asked us a lot of questions and was quite knowledgeable.*
  - *Bill was a fantastic course leader. He was incredibly personable and made us feel comfortable throughout. I would highly recommend Bill in the future.*
  - *Bill was absolutely fantastic. He was engaging, incredibly informed and had a relaxed yet professional style. He made us comfortable in asking questions and went at the pace we needed.*
  - *Extremely professional, one of the best presenters to date.*

Option Six: Conversations About Suicide

Do you know how to help a suicidal person – with awareness and compassion?

Learn practical skills to improve your confidence to provide mental health first aid to someone who is feeling suicidal.

This training consists of 4 hours face-to-face workshop or online interactive workshop via Zoom, and course participants receive a handbook and online Certificate of Completion.

The 4-hour Mental Health First Aid - Conversations about Suicide course is for any interested adult.

You will learn the skills and acquire the knowledge required to safely have a conversation with a person who may be experiencing suicidal thoughts and behaviours.

This course is based on guidelines developed through the expert consensus of people with lived experience of mental health problems.

The curriculum content is evidence-based, with the input of both mental health professionals, researchers and consumer advocates - 'Suicidal Thoughts and Behaviours: First Aid Guidelines'.

This training complements the 12-hour Standard MHFA course and the 14-hour Youth MHFA course. Who can attend? Any interested adult can attend.

This course is not a therapy or support group or a postvention course, rather it is an education course and it is important that people undertaking the course are feeling relatively robust when they undertake it.

It is not recommended for individuals recently bereaved by suicide.

Option Seven: Additional Workshops

You can find out more about all my additional workshops and training opportunities via the QR code on the back cover. This chart offers a quick-reference guide to what's available.

BILL CARSON - WORKSHOPS

Please scan the QR code on the back cover for details and free resources

	WORKSHOP
1.1	Mental Health First Aid – Accreditation Training
1.2	Mental Health First Aid - Refresher training
2	Resilience & Wellbeing First Aid – Accreditation Training
3	S.A.F.E Conversation Skills for Work and Life™
4	Skilful Communication for Managers to Handle Issues of Change, Motivation and Performance
5	Personal Best Leadership Training
6	Strategies for Handling Issues such as Change & Disruption & Conflict
7	Personal Strategies for Work & Life Challenges to Strengthen Happiness and Success
8	Thriving Through Turbulent Times
9	Energise & Empower - Wellbeing and Mental Health Skills for Managers and Teams

FREE BONUS RESOURCES

To enjoy even more benefits from this book, we invite you to sign up to **www.inspirelearning.au**

Please scan the QR code below or type this website into your browser.

Here you will find links to free resources and membership to continue developing your person-centred skills and additional resources to support your growth and development.

ABOUT THE AUTHOR

Bill Carson brings expertise in mental health and resilience as a Principal Master Instructor of Mental Health First Aid and Certified Resilience Instructor to organisations in Australia in the following industries: retail, legal, manufacturing, healthcare, advertising, and aged and community care. Bill is also a regular volunteer Lifeline Telephone Crisis Supporter with over 650 hours experience.

Bill Carson also has over 20 years of experience and expertise in sales, marketing, management, service culture, business development, key account management, facilitation and personal development coaching across a wide range of industries (manufacturing, professional services, banking and finance, insurance, ITC, healthcare and retail).

His long list of achievements never indicated what was happening beneath the surface.

Through a lived experience of over 30 years' suffering, 'hiding' and overcoming his own depression and anxiety, Bill now blends his personal and professional expertise into developing well-being, mental health and resilience solutions for professionals.

Bill's Areas of Expertise

- Mental Health First Aid, Principal Master Instructor
- Well-being Skills & Resilience Skills Coaching
- Social and Emotional Intelligence Coaching
- Executive Coaching
- Train the Trainer and Presentation Skills
- Lifeline Volunteer Telephone Crisis Support
- Leadership, Organisational Culture & Values
- Personal Development
- Team Alignment and Interpersonal Skills

- Sales Training, Sales Coaching, Sales Management and Negotiation Skills
- Customer Service Excellence, Call Centres and Service Management

Bill's Qualifications

- Bachelor of Science in Metallurgy from Melbourne University
- Diploma of Management – BSB51107
- Adult Education and Certificate IV – Training and Assessment – TAE 40110
- Certified Coach and Master Trainer in Sales, Leadership and Service
- Accredited Mental Health First Aid Principal Master Instructor
- Accredited Resilience Coach, Well-being Coach and Social & Emotional Intelligence Coach
- Certified Neuroscience of Coaching
- Executive Coaching – ICCP (Sydney University)

GRATITUDE

The following people have made profound and significant contributions to my life – both personally and professionally.

- My darling wife Lee-Anne Carson, wonderful son Richard Carson, my family – Helen, Peter, Tom, Paul, Leanne and Maree, and their children and partners. My parents Richard Carson, Elisabeth Crooks and Alan Crooks. My first wife Lorraine Carson.
- Greg Dixon and Linny Hursthouse, Michael Harris, Robyn Henderson
- The HSE Global team
- The Mental Health First Aid Australia team
- The Lifeline team – John, Donna, Jim, Michael, Andrew
- Carli Phillips, Marianne Dodds, John Smibert, Jurie Rossouw, Corrina Lindby, Karen Chasten, Litsa Barberoglou, Tom Verghese, Christina Foxwell, Ron Allen, Dr David Keane, Simone Allan
- Alan and Cathie Hilton, Alex Girard, Geoff Dunleavy, Darren Muir, Gabrielle Sumner, Ben Docherty, Brett Hainsworth, Fraser Batts, Jason Lunn, Amanda McNaughton, Trevor McIntyre
- Jason Murray and Andy Springer, Bob Coulthurst, Darryl Fayers
- Audrey McGibbon and the GLWS team, Susan Gardiner, Heidi Denning, Suzie Dafnis and Peter Johnston
- Dale and Pam Richardson, Alan Bassal and Shoshana Faire, Mark and Glenys Curry, Dan and Muffy Churches
- Authors, teachers, speakers, leaders – Dr Daniel Amen, Dr Gabor Mate, Dr Brene Brown, Simon Sinek, Dr Adam Fraser, Dr Ed Hess, Dr Dan Seigel, the leaders of the many wisdom traditions that I have explored
- The Banksia Guys – Geoff, Shay, Stephen, Phil, Larry, John, Scott, David

REFERENCES

Deloitte, *Well-being and Resilience in Senior Leaders, A Playbook for Action,* (Published 2 August 2022)

Mental Health First Aid Manual, p.4, 4th Edition March 2022

Daniel Siegal, Aware, (New York, TarcherPerigee, 2020)

Jim Clifton and Jim Harter, *Well-being at Work, (New York,* Gallup, 2012)

Gallup, World's Negative Experience Index, *Gallup's latest Negative Experience Index, which annually tracks these experiences worldwide in more than 100 countries and areas, shows that collectively, the world was feeling the worst it had in 15 years. The index score reached a new high of 32 in 2020.*

Bev Aisbett, *The Book of Burnout,* (Australia, Harper Collins, 2023)

Gill Hasson and Donna Butler, *Mental Health and Wellbeing in the Workplace,* (Great Britain, Wiley, 2020)

John Gray, *Staying Focused in a Hyper World,* (JG Publications 2014)

Daniel Amen, *Change Your Brain, Change Your Life (Great Britain , Piatkus, 2010)*

William Walsh, *Nutrient Power* (New York, Skyhorse, 2014)

Adam Grant, *Give and Take: A Revolutionary Approach to Success* (New York: Viking Press, 2013)

Bessel Van Der Kolk, *The Body Keeps Score, (United Kingdom, Penguin, 2015)*

Stephen Pinker, *Enlightenment Now, the tone of the news 1945-2010, p.51 (Penguin UK, 2018)*

Brene Brown, *The Gifts of Imperfection (USA, Hazelden, 2010)*

Donna Jackson Nakazawa, *Childhood Disrupted (New York, Atria, 2018) How Your Biography Becomes Your Biology, and How You Can Heal* created a survey to determine the likelihood of Adverse Childhood Experiences.

Susan David, *Emotional Agility*, (Great Britain Penguin, 2016)

Prof. Tony Jorm & Dr. Alyssia Rosetto, *Developing a model of help-giving towards people with a mental health problem* (University of Melbourne, 2015)

Paul Gilbert, *The Compassionate Mind* (Great Britain, Robinson, 2013)

Jurie Rossouw, *Executive Resilience*, (Sydney, RForce, 2017)

Patrick Holford, *Optimum Nutrition for the Brain* (Great Britain, Piatkus Books, 2007)

Neuroscience of Mindfulness Meditation in 4 minutes - https://www.youtube.com/watch?v=vo_VANW35b0
https://hbr.org/2015/01/mindfulness-can-literally-change-your-brain

Luthans, F., Vogelgesang, G. R., & Lester, P. B. (2006). Developing the psychological capital of resiliency. Human Resource Development Review, 5(1), 25-44.

Blau, G. (2017). The relationships among personality, coping strategies, and job stress in a sample of managers. Journal of Managerial Psychology, 32(1), 51-65.

Burke, R. J., & Richardsen, A. M. (2016). Occupational health psychology: Work, stress, and health. Routledge.

Amagoh, F. (2009). Leadership development and leadership effectiveness. Management Decision, 47(6), 989-999.

Decety, J., & Cowell, J. M. (2014). Friends or foes: is empathy necessary for moral behavior?. Perspectives on psychological science, 9(5), 525-537.

Davis, M. H. (1996). Empathy: A social psychological approach. Westview Press.

Lelorain, S., Brédart, A., & Dolbeault, S. (2012). A systematic review of the associations between empathy measures and patient outcomes in cancer care. Psycho Oncology, 21(12), 1255-1264.

Schuch FB, et al. Exercise for depression: A systematic review and meta-analysis. American Journal of Psychiatry. 2018;175(7): 631-648.

Stubbs B, et al. Physical activity and mental health: A review of the literature. Journal of Affective Disorders. 2017; 245: 86-92.

Mikkelsen K, et al. Exercise and mental health. Maturitas. 2017;106: 48-56.

Cotman CW, Berchtold NC. Exercise: a behavioral intervention to enhance brain health and plasticity. Trends in Neuroscience. 2002;25(6): 295-301.

Kandola A, et al. Physical activity and depression: Towards understanding the antidepressant mechanisms of physical activity. Neuroscience and Biobehavioral Reviews. 2019;107: 525-539.

SAFE CONVERSATIONS FOR WORK AND LIFE™